6 CHAPTERS in DESIGN

SAUL BASS

IVAN CHERMAYEFF

MILTON GLASER

PAUL RAND

IKKO TANAKA

HENRYK TOMASZEWSKI

Foreword by Philip B. Meggs

CHRONICLE BOOKS
SAN FRANCISCO

First published by
Chronicle Books in 1997.

Originally published as six separate hardcover volumes under the series title *World Graphic Design* by Ginza Graphic Gallery, Tokyo, Japan.

Printed in Hong Kong.

ISBN: 0-8118-1722-9

Library of Congress
Cataloging-in-Publication Data available.

Cover and text design: Carole Goodman

Distributed in Canada by
Raincoast Books
8680 Cambie Street
Vancouver, B.C. V6P 6M9

10 9 8 7 6 5 4 3 2

Chronicle Books
85 Second Street
San Francisco, California 94105

www.chroniclebooks.com

TABLE OF CONTENTS

FOREWORD

by PHILIP B. MEGGS

FROM THE RANKS OF THOUSANDS OF GRAPHIC DESIGNERS WHO PRODUCE VISUAL COMMUNICATIONS OF VALUE TO THEIR CLIENTS AND THE PUBLIC, A FEW EMERGE AS UNIQUE ARTISTS WHOSE BODY OF WORK EXPANDS THE POTENTIAL OF CREATIVE DESIGN. WHAT SEPARATES A MASTER FROM THE CORPS OF TALENTED DESIGNERS? A PERSONAL CREATIVE VISION, A UNIQUE APPROACH TO PROBLEM-SOLVING, AND A DISTINCTIVE LEXICON OF VISUAL FORMS—THESE ATTRIBUTES LEAD TO WORKS WHOSE AUTHORSHIP IS IMMEDIATELY RECOGNIZABLE. DESIGNS BY A MASTER PERMEATE THE INFORMATION ENVIRONMENT AND REVERBERATE AS A DISTINCTIVE INFLUENCE WITHIN THE CULTURE.

The Ginza Graphic Gallery in Tokyo initiated a series of one-person exhibitions by outstanding graphic designers, and has published a delightful small-format book about each featured artist. Chronicle Books has collected six of

these volumes into this substantial edition, laden with innovative graphics by six masters in the field.

Six Chapters in Design celebrates the accomplishments of a half-dozen designers whose work has had an indelible influence on the evolution of design in our time. Each "chapter" developed over a lifetime of confronting a blank sheet of paper and a specific problem in need of a graphic solution. All six of these designers evolved a singular ability to breathe life into the white void of the untouched paper—out of emptiness creating a personal artistic statement *and* a public message.

The chapter of graphic design by Saul Bass is about a pioneer who built a reputation for graphic design in the American West. During the 1940s, the East Coast dominated graphic design. Bass moved from New York to Los Angeles, where he developed an uncanny ability to seize the essence of complex messages and express them through elemental glyphs. This ability led to parallel accomplishments in several design arenas, from instantly recognizable trademarks for major corporations to his legendary film titles. He reinvented the film title by letting symbols, words, and images perform a cinematic ballet in time and space. Works of art in themselves, his cinematic titles perfectly capture the mood and spirit of the motion picture.

Ivan Chermayeff vaporized the inviolate walls between art and public communications. His design partnership,

Chermayeff and Geismar, has remained at the forefront of visual identity and corporate literature for over forty years. As if these accomplishments were not enough, Chermayeff has pursued a parallel career making tapestries, posters, children's books, and fine-art collages. The method behind these works is a casual and spirited use of collage and montage, ranging from the scruffiness of discarded ephemera to the purity of brightly colored papers. Chermayeff, like Bass, produces works whose authorship is as identifiable as a Bach concerto.

The third chapter presents works by Milton Glaser, who attained the stature of a cult figure in the design world in the 1960s. Rather than rest on his laurels, Glaser has remained a restless risk taker, opening doors, windows, and closets, experimenting with media and inventing new ways to combine and recombine images. Glaser mines the whole of visual culture for inspiration, then reinvents the raw material into superlative expressions of his own vision. In his chapter, printed designs are accompanied by preliminary studies. Design is a process of searching and seeking; a master such as Glaser will develop sketch after sketch in his search for a magical image that dramatically transcends the ordinary.

America was long an artistic banana republic, a cultural outpost of Europe. Paul Rand ranks high among the American designers who used European modernism, not as a model to be emulated, but as a springboard to launch

into new directions. Rand understands the duality of color and form. They have an intrinsic artistic life as perceptual energy, while also functioning as signs or symbols bearing a message to the viewer. Rand's mastery of this duality permitted him to solve pragmatic communications assignments with vitality and force. Works he created five decades ago remain alive and dynamic long after the need for the client's message has passed. Most other designs from earlier decades are now lifeless and wilted, because their creators did not understand or generate the visual energy of Rand's designs.

The first four chapters present works that were "made in the U.S.A."; they are followed by a chapter highlighting the works of Japanese designer Ikko Tanaka. He grounds his work in elemental geometric form. Geometry is usually considered to be universal, impersonal, and inert. In the hands of an artist with Tanaka's imagination and feeling, timeless and universal geometry is imbued with a rare poetry. Shape is his medium. Colored slivers of circles combine with squares and rectangles to create portraits conveying character and feeling. Diamonds become eyes; circles become astounded mouths. Butterflies flutter and books fly. Calligraphy is placed on vibrant blocks of color. Tanaka shows how the worlds of public message and private art can be integrated, simultaneously serving the needs of audience, client, and designer.

Henryk Tomaszewski, widely respected for leading a

revival of postwar Polish design through his posters and teaching, is presented in Chapter Six. Behind the simplicity and spontaneity of Tomaszewski's posters is an analytical search for just the right image or symbol to project the essence of the subject. His informal gesture drawings camouflage careful analysis and meticulous adjustment of every nuance. The assured movement of his hand generates energy and confidence. His unerring sense of placement and balance lends refinement to his work, demonstrating a rightness to the whole. Words in Tomaszewski posters are often part of the drawing. His lettering ranges from brash brush calligraphy to jittery pen scrawls and meticulous yet decidedly handmade printing; it expresses the content and complements the image. Centrally placed, his iconic images have presence and authority.

These *Six Chapters in Design* prove that the long struggle for recognition as a profession—and for acknowledgment of design's artistic and social value—has yielded fruit. The blossoming of talents of this magnitude allows graphic design to stand with more traditional art forms as a major attainment of human culture.

1

SAUL bass

saul bass

A COMBINATION OF INTELLECT & EMOTION

by LOUIS DORFSMAN, graphic designer

DISCIPLINED CREATIVITY—THE INTENSIVE IN-DEPTH EXPLORATION OF AN ISSUE, SUBJECT, PROBLEM. THE INCLUSION OF COMMON SENSE AND UNCOMMON INSIGHTS . . . RELEVANCE AND APPROPRIATENESS . . . INFUSING THE WHOLE THROUGH A VISION, BOTH LITERARY AND VISUAL, WITH RESULTS THAT SURPASS ONE'S EXPECTATIONS FOR INNOVATIVE AND IMAGINATIVE SOLUTIONS. THAT SUMS UP THE DESIGN PHENOMENON THAT IS THE LATE SAUL BASS.

Saul Bass practiced his craft and his magic for more than fifty years, yet his work was always consistently "new" and provocative, and always of the moment. His work remains relevant because it continues to touch people and because his ideas and his imagery appeal as much to the emotions as they do to the intellect.

This combination of intellect and emotion (one might call them the yin and yang of design), came through in

everything Bass touched, whether it was a packaging program, a poster for a film festival, an extensive corporate identity program for United Airlines or AT&T, or a gasoline station in South America, Europe, or Japan.

It is not possible to discuss Saul Bass's contributions and not include a few observations about the "other" side of Saul, the film side. A well-documented fact is that Saul "invented," virtually single-handedly, a new breed of filmtitling in the sixties.

In addition to his work on titles, Saul directed a feature film and several short films—most often in collaboration with his wife Elaine Bass. He received an Academy Award for his film *Why Man Creates*, while several of his other films have received nominations.

The hard fact is that the work presented here simply scratches the surface of Saul Bass's endeavors over the years. The vast scope of his extraordinary creative output is merely hinted at . . . but you'll get the idea!

saul bass

AS A DESIGNER OF FILMS

by MARTIN SCORSESE, film director

SAUL BASS'S REPUTATION AS A DESIGNER OF FILM IS LEGENDARY. HE HAS LEFT HIS INDELIBLE SIGNATURE ON A NUMBER OF PICTURES BY PREMINGER, HITCHCOCK, KUBRICK, AND WYLER, AMONG OTHERS.

It was exciting growing up on movies during the 1950s and 1960s. The "growing" entailed a great deal of learning, too. Part of that excitement and learning was due to the remarkable contribution of Saul Bass in some of the greatest films of those periods—from *The Man with the Golden Arm* to *North by Northwest* to *Psycho* to *Spartacus*, and beyond.

Saul Bass fashioned title sequences into an art, creating in some cases, like *Vertigo*, a mini-film within a film. His graphic compositions in movement function as a prologue to the movie—setting the tone, providing the mood, and foreshadowing the action.

His titles are not simply unimaginative identification tags, as in many films; rather, they are integral to the film as a whole. When his work comes up on the screen, the movie itself truly begins.

I had the honor and the opportunity to work with Saul and Elaine Bass on four of my pictures—*Goodfellas*, *Cape Fear*, *The Age of Innocence*, and *Casino*.

It had been a dream of mine to work with Saul Bass ever since I tried to capture his style on my own imaginary movie titles that I drew at ages twelve and fifteen in a composition book I kept hidden at home. I feel very fortunate to have had that dream realized.

THE MAGNIFICENT SEVEN · DIRECTED BY JOHN STURGES

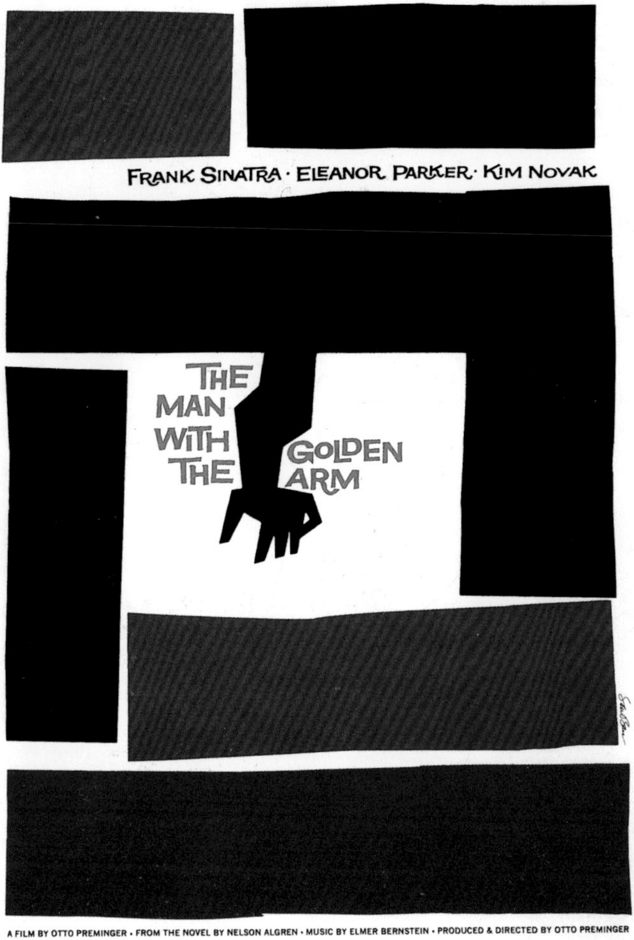
FRANK SINATRA · ELEANOR PARKER · KIM NOVAK
THE MAN WITH THE GOLDEN ARM
A FILM BY OTTO PREMINGER · FROM THE NOVEL BY NELSON ALGREN · MUSIC BY ELMER BERNSTEIN · PRODUCED & DIRECTED BY OTTO PREMINGER

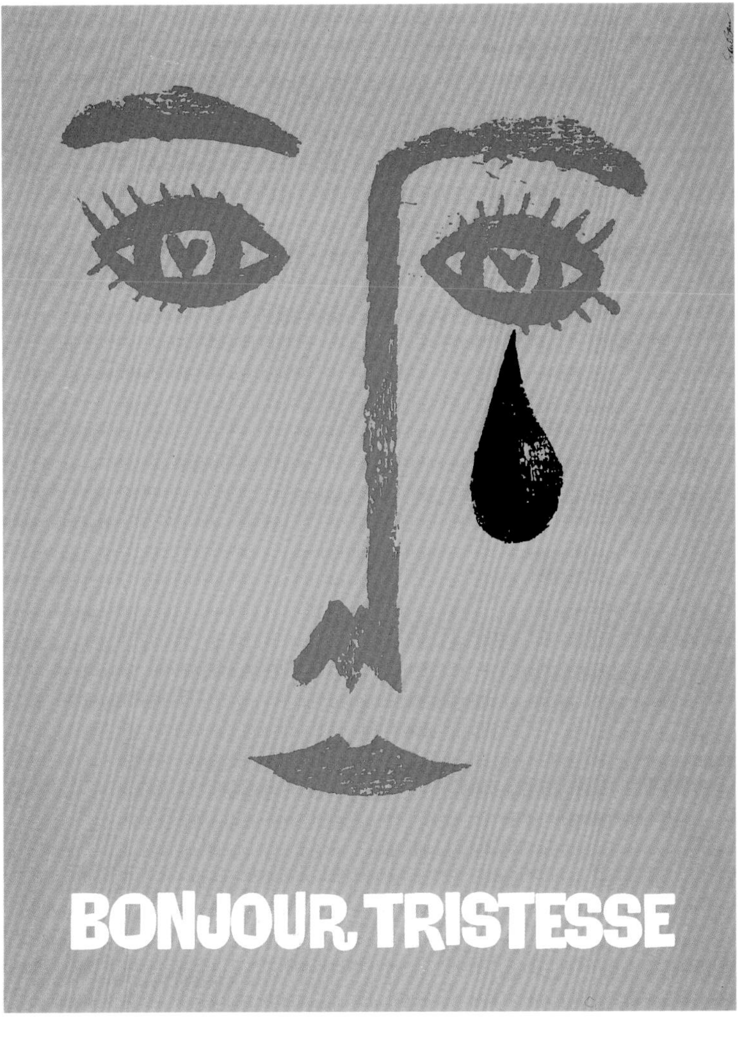
BONJOUR, TRISTESSE

24

SAINT JOAN
OTTO PREMINGER PRESENTS BERNARD SHAWS SAINT JOAN STARRING RICHARD WIDMARK RICHARD TODD ANTON WALBROOK JOHN GIELGUD & JEAN SEBERG

OTTO PREMINGER PRESENTS
ADVISE & CONSENT
HENRY FONDA, CHARLES LAUGHTON, DON MURRAY, WALTER PIDGEON, PETER LAWFORD, GENE TIERNEY, LEW AYRES, FRANCHOT TONE, BURGESS MEREDITH, EDDIE HODGES, PAUL FORD, GEORGE GRIZZARD, INGA SWENSON
SCREENPLAY WRITTEN BY WENDELL MAYES, MUSIC BY JERRY FIELDING, PHOTOGRAPHED IN PANAVISION BY SAM LEAVITT, PRODUCED AND DIRECTED BY OTTO PREMINGER, A COLUMBIA PICTURES RELEASE

25

Starring James Stewart/Lee Remick/Ben Gazzara/Arthur O'Connell/Eve Arden/Kathryn Grant and Joseph N. Welch as Judge Weaver/With George C. Scott/Orson Bean/Murray Hamilton
Screenplay by Wendell Mayes/Photography by Sam Leavitt/Production designed by Boris Leven Music by Duke Ellington/Produced and Directed by Otto Preminger/A Columbia release

EXODUS

A JOHN FRANKENHEIMER FILM IN CINERAMA

STARRING

JAMES GARNER · EVA MARIE SAINT · YVES MONTAND
TOSHIRO MIFUNE · BRIAN BEDFORD · JESSICA WALTERS
ANTONIO SABATO · FRANCOISE HARDY · ADOLFO CELI

Directed by John Frankenheimer · Produced by Edward Lewis

SUCH GOOD FRIENDS

30

Directed by Claude Berri with Michel Simon and Alain Cohen • A Cinema V presentation

THE SHINING
A STANLEY KUBRICK FILM · STARRING JACK NICHOLSON AND SHELLEY DUVALL
WITH SCATMAN CROTHERS, DANNY LLOYD, BARRY NELSON AND PHILLIP STONE
PRODUCED & DIRECTED BY STANLEY KUBRICK · BASED ON THE NOVEL BY STEPHEN KING

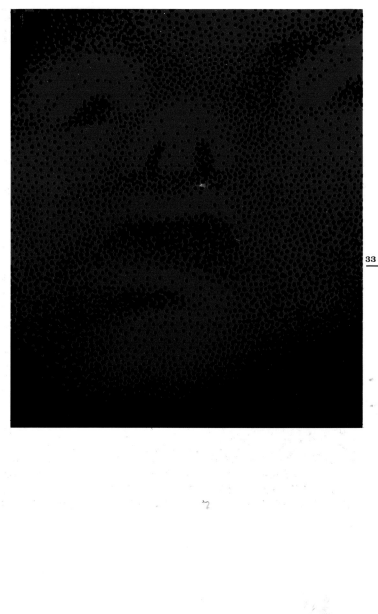

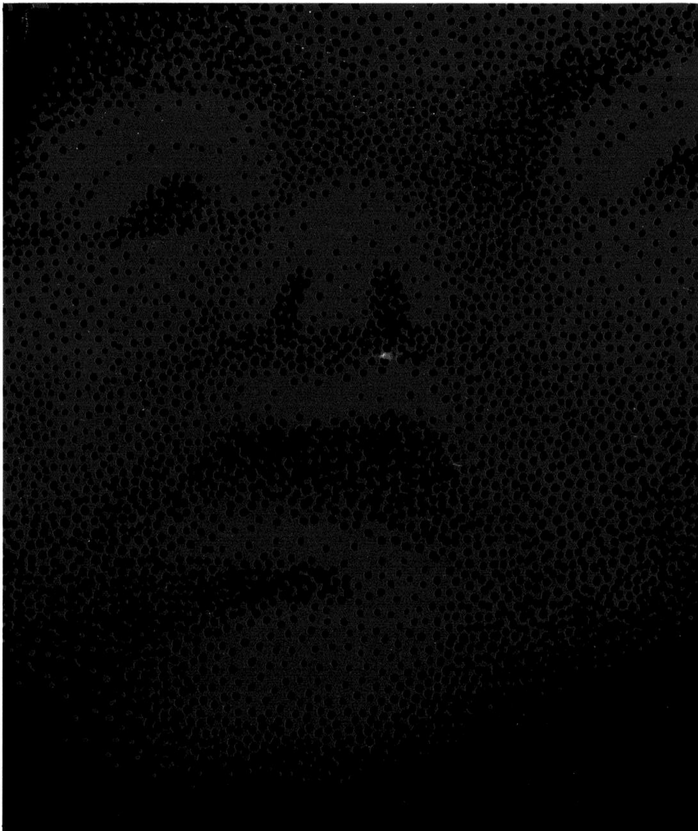

33

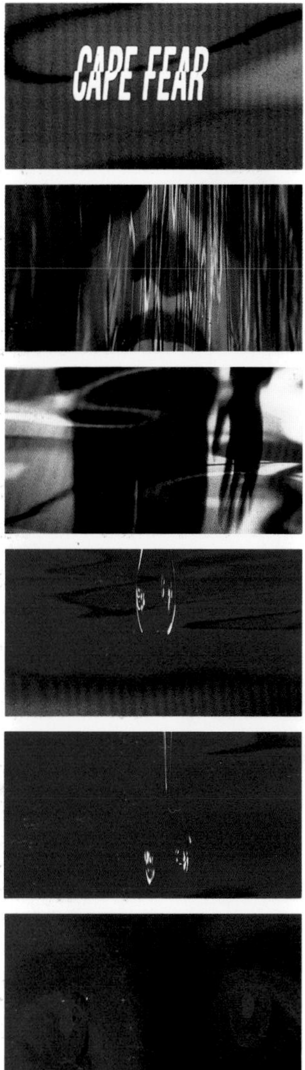
CAPE FEAR

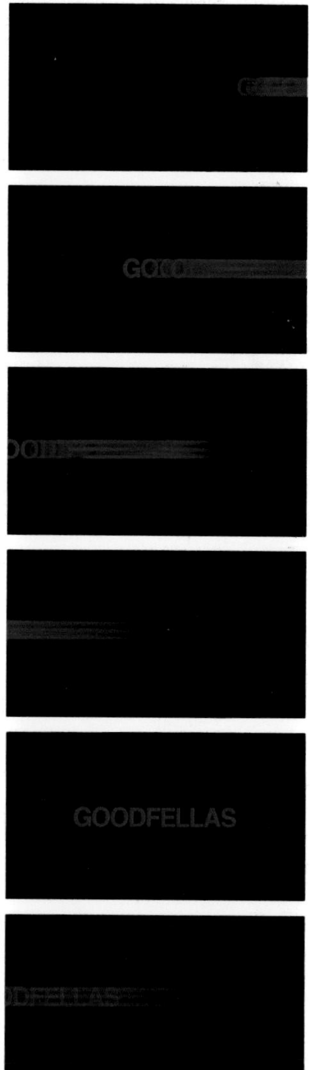
GOODFELLAS

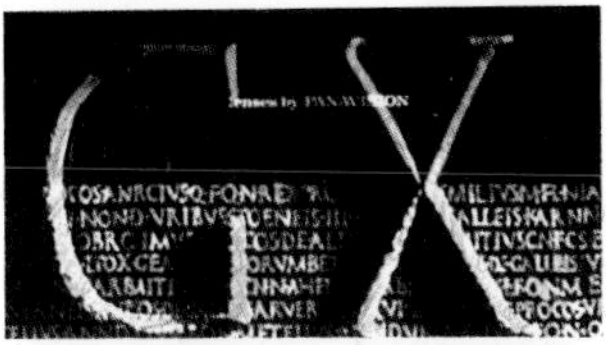

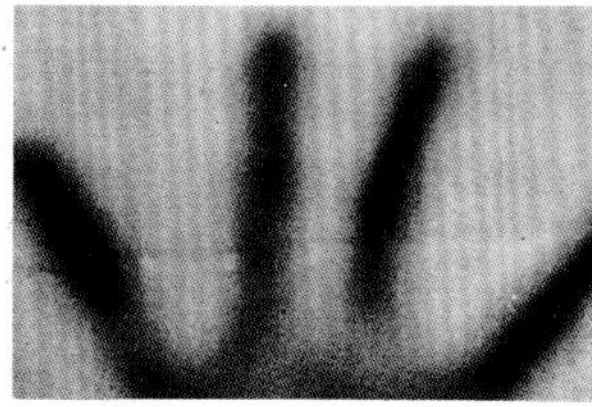
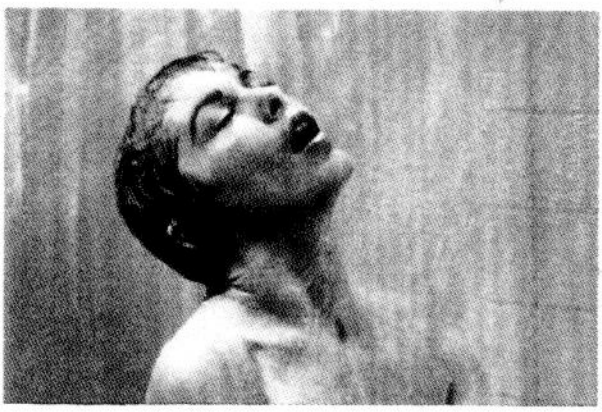

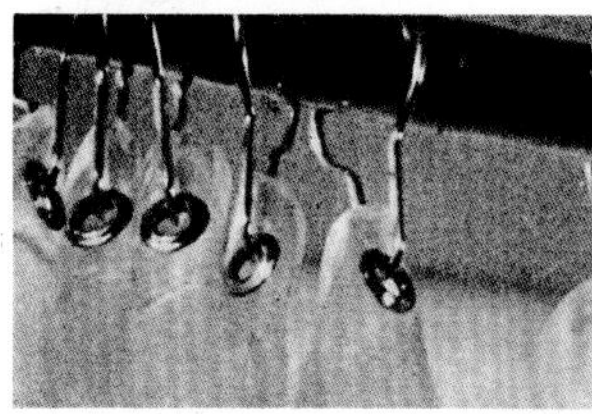
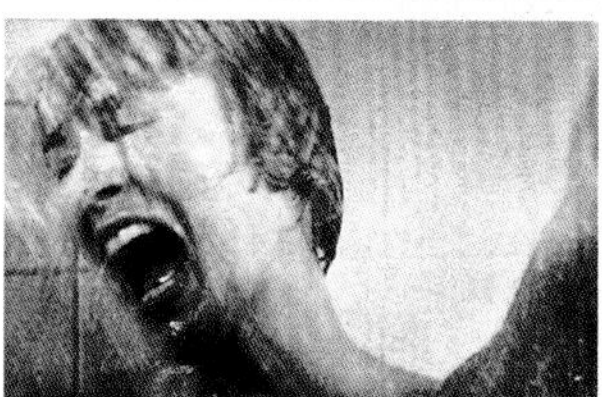
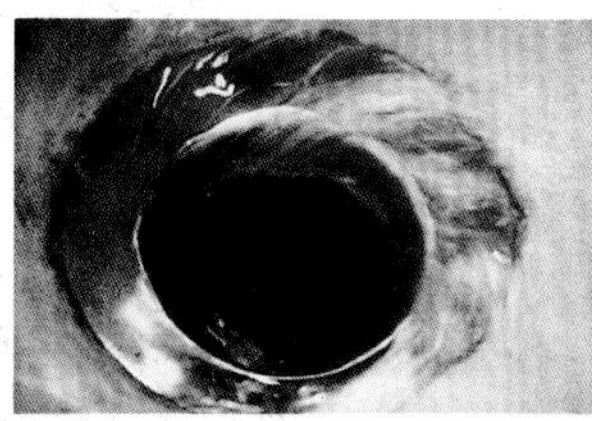

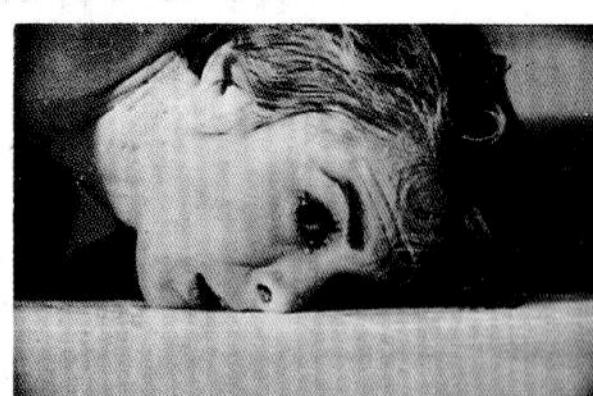

F MARCH
I 14-28
L 1985
M
E
X

10th Chicago
International
Film Festival
1974

1936
1986
Directors
Guild of
America
Golden
Jubilee

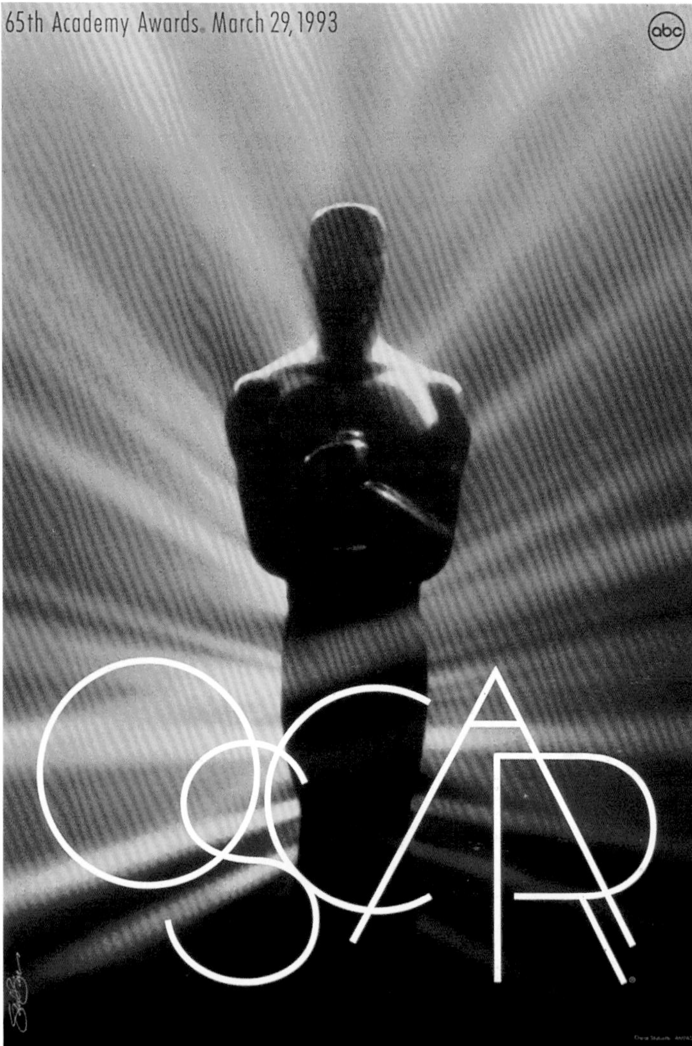
65th Academy Awards. March 29, 1993
abc
OSCAR

Games of the XXIIIrd Olympiad Los Angeles 1984
SIGNATURE SERIES / DESIGNED BY SAUL BASS

Human Rights
1789-1989
ges Internationales pour les Droits de l'Homme et du Citoyen
ARTIS 89

CONDUCTORS: JERZY MAKSYMIUK & YEHUDI MENUHIN

UCLA EXTENSION
75th Year Anniversary

PSYCHOLOGY
Harper & Row

47

PSYCHOLOGY
Third Edition / Harper Collins
Carole Wade & Carol Tavris

48

PSYCHOLOGY
Third Edition / Harper Collins
Carole Wade & Carol Tavris

49

54

AT&T

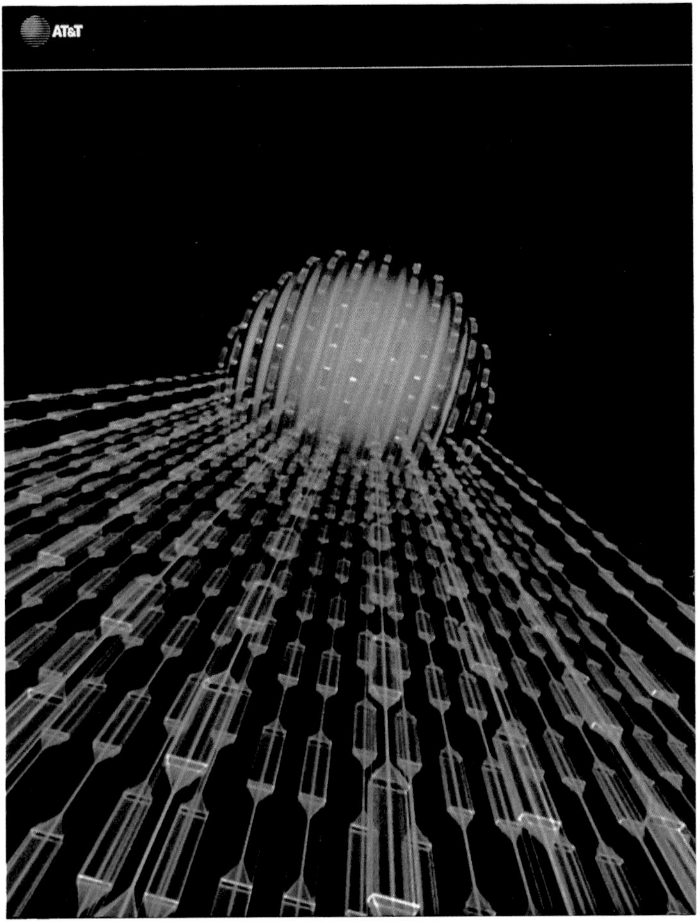
AT&T

N4710U

LAWRY'S
SEASONED

EXXON
EXXON
Self
EXXON
Self
EXXON
Cashier
Car Care

BP

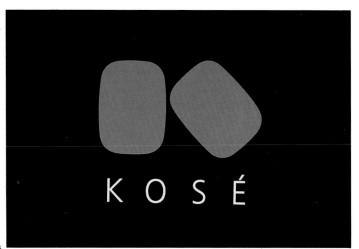

KOSÉ

Minami

KIBUN

MINOLTA

GIRL SCOUTS

JOMO

Saul Bass was born in New York in 1920. He worked in many roles as art director, designer, photographer, illustrator, and filmmaker. Bass reinvented film-credit titles and created titles for over forty motion pictures, including ANATOMY OF A MURDER, WALK ON THE WILD SIDE, AROUND THE WORLD IN 80 DAYS, MAN WITH THE GOLDEN ARM, VERTIGO, NORTH BY NORTHWEST, WEST SIDE STORY, CAPE FEAR, GOODFELLAS, THE AGE OF INNOCENCE, CASINO, and others. He directed the racing sequences in GRAND PRIX and the shower sequence in PSYCHO, as well as others. In addition, he helped Stanley Kubrick design the final battle sequence in SPARTACUS. He also directed many short films, some of which have received awards, including the Grand Award at the Venice Film Festival, an Oscar for WHY MAN CREATES, and a Gold Medal at the Moscow Film Festival for QUEST. In 1974 he directed the feature film PHASE IV.

Bass designed numerous trademarks and corporate identity programs for such companies as AT&T, United Airlines, Minolta, General Foods, Celanese, Quaker Oats, Rockwell International, Boys Clubs, Girl Scouts, and Japan Energy Corporation.

His work is held in the permanent collections of the Museum of Modern Art, New York; the Library of Congress; the Prague Museum, Czechoslovakia; the Stedelijk Museum, Amsterdam; and the Israel Museum, Jerusalem. He was a founding trustee of the Sundance Film Institute, a member of the board of governors for the Academy of Motion Pictures Arts & Sciences, a co-director of the Aspen International Design Conference, and a member of the National Humanities Faculty. He died in 1996.

AWARDS AND HONORS

Bass was an honorary member of the Royal Designers for Industry, Royal Society of Arts, England. He received a citation for Distinction Brought to the Profession from the Philadelphia Museum of Art. He was inducted into the New York Art Directors Club Hall of Fame in 1977 and was the recipient of an AIGA Gold Medal. He also received many other awards.

2

IVAN chermayeff

IVAN CHERMAYEFF

by HENRY WOLF, graphic designer

THE RECIPE IS COMPLEX AND NOT ALWAYS EASILY AVAILABLE TO THE MASSES. TAKE A CURIOUS YOUNG BOY, THE SON OF A RUSSIAN FATHER—A FAMOUS ARCHITECT—AND AN ENGLISH MOTHER, AND LET HIM LIVE IN ENGLAND BETWEEN THE WARS, SURROUNDED IN HIS EARLY YEARS BY THE LUMINARIES OF INTER-NATIONAL DESIGN AND ARCHITECTURE. THEN TRANSPLANT HIM TO THE UNITED STATES. AND KEEP the same privileged circumstances intact, but with some Eastern establishment flavor added. Let him hang around the Art Institute of Chicago, send him to Harvard, and by the time he's grown up you have the possibility of getting someone like Ivan Chermayeff. No guarantee, but a good chance. You still need the boyish good looks, the slightly frayed London-tailored overcoats, the self-deprecating humor, and, most importantly, the gifted eyes and the

self-confidence that make his work look so effortless and never labored, so varied in its range from hard-lined geometric logos to loose and child-like illustrations.

I have known and often worked with Ivan for around thirty-five years, and I am still amazed at the ease with which he switches from designing an annual report to creating a huge three-dimensional sculpture, like the free-standing number 9 on 57th Street, to writing and illustrating a children's book. Maybe my admiration stems from my jealousy toward someone who is not as frozen in his ways as I am.

As Ivan's work progresses, it acquires more freedom and bolder, brighter colors, becoming more art than discipline. And yet he is an excellent typographer and a very lucid writer, or is it the other way around?

If I didn't like him so much, the temptation to burn down his studio might become irresistible. But it would also be senseless because, knowing Ivan, out of all the ashes would come even better, more colorful, more essential work.

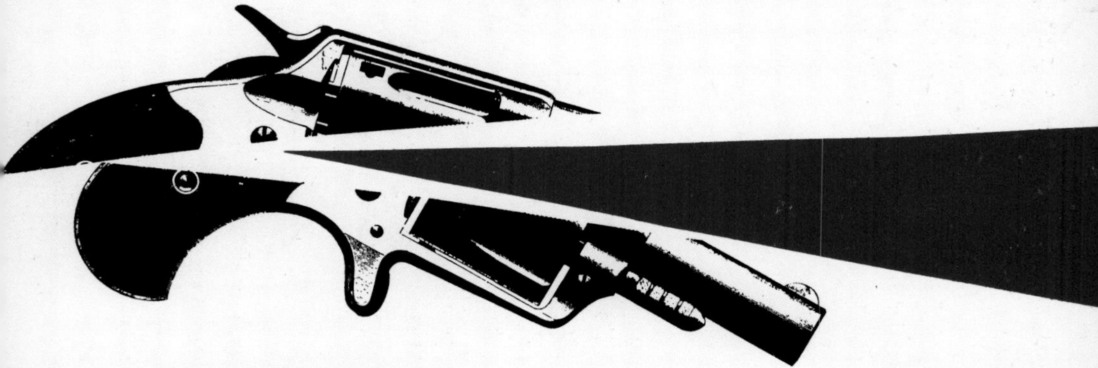

1958 PEACE CALENDAR

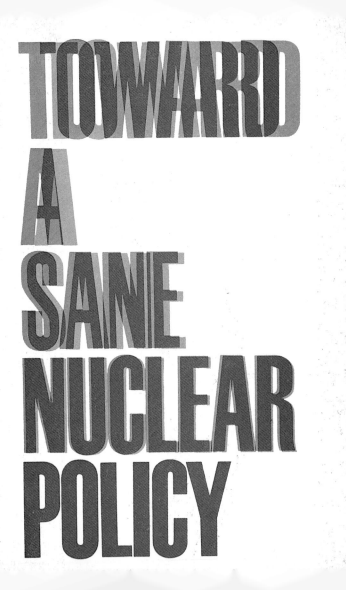

TOWARD A SANE NUCLEAR POLICY

Ivan Chermayeff
The Museum of Broadcasting
celebrates
Mobil Masterpiece Theatre
15 years of excellence
A retrospective exhibition
January 24 - April 4, 1986
1 East 53rd Street
MB
MUSEUM OF BROADCASTING
Mobil

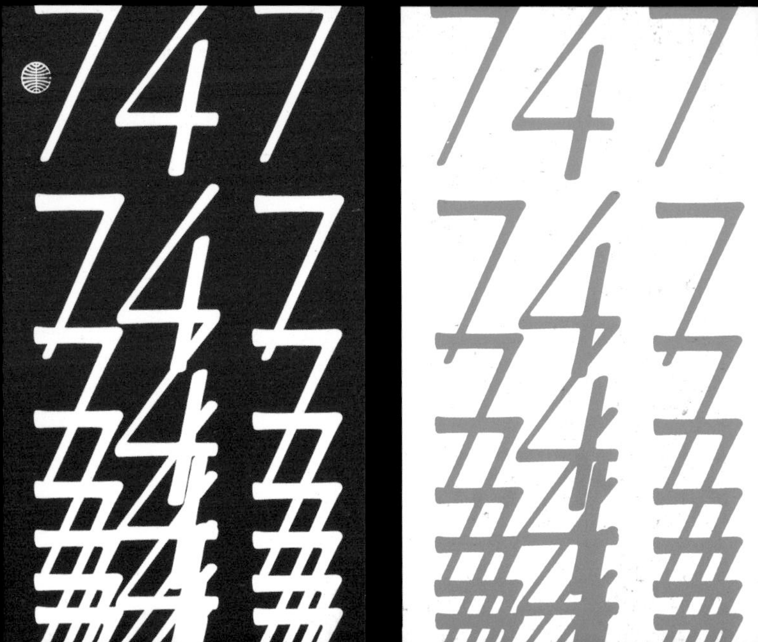
747
747

The Bolshoi Ballet

Jacob's Pillow 1993
Ivan Chermayeff

Tomato and Other Colors Ivan Chermayeff

Anthony Davis
The Ghost Factory
Kansas City Symphony Orchestra
Conducted by William McGlaughlin
Shem Guibbory, Violin

Sun Moon Star
Kurt Vonnegut & Ivan Chermayeff

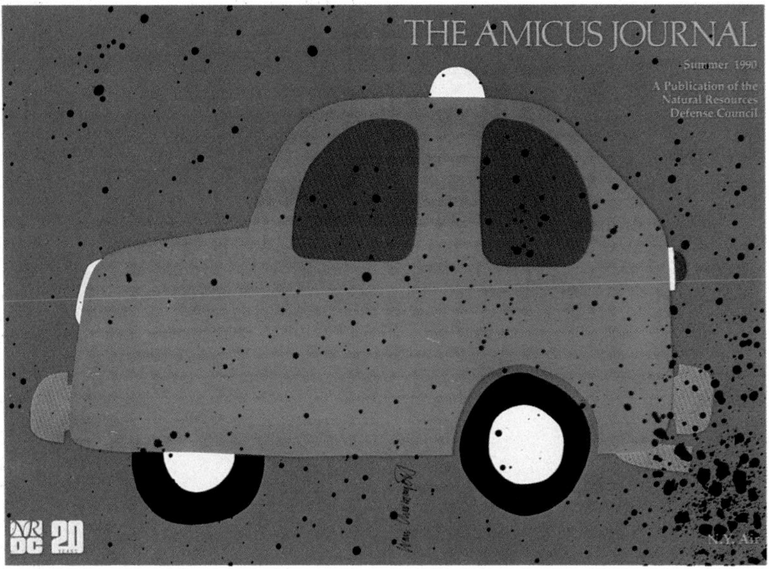
THE AMICUS JOURNAL
Summer 1990
A Publication of the
Natural Resources
Defense Council
NRDC
20
N.Y. Air

Think
THE IBM MAGAZINE
NUMBER 1/1991

BIG
APPLE
CIRCUS
New York's very own circus in a magical all new show with the Nanjing Acrobatic Troupe at Lincoln Center Oct. 27–Jan. 2
WCBS
88

a

b

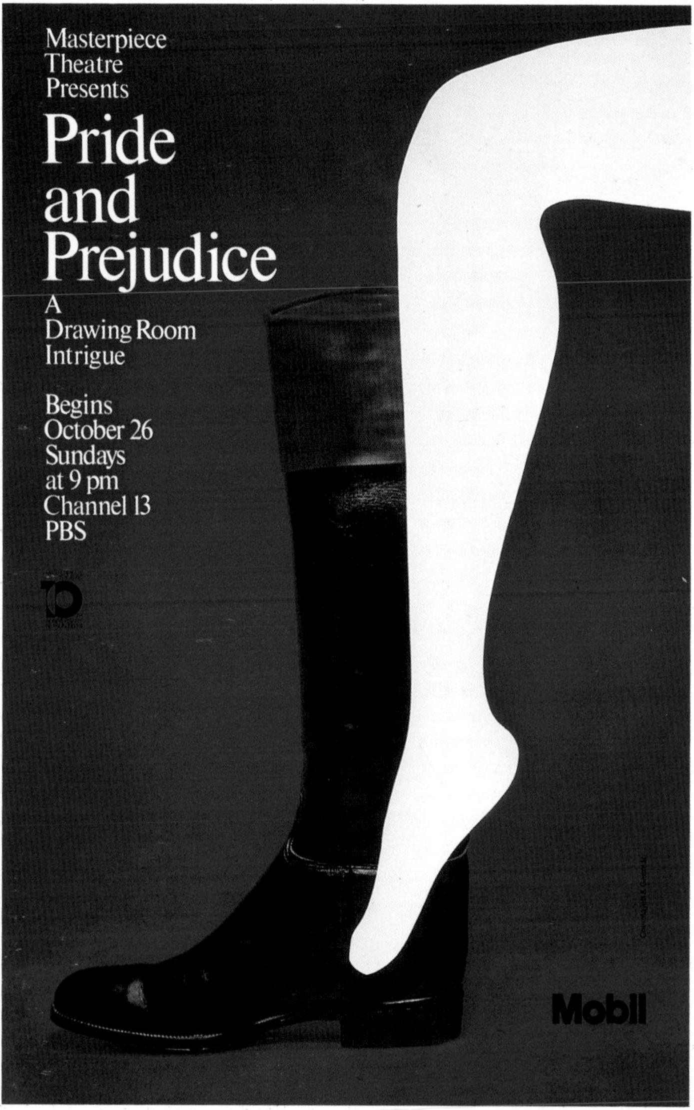
Masterpiece
Theatre
Presents
Pride
and
Prejudice
A
Drawing Room
Intrigue
Begins
October 26
Sundays
at 9 pm
Channel 13
PBS
Mobil

Honoré de Balzac's

'Sweet Cousin Bette'
thought only of her family-
and their destruction

Mobil Masterpiece Theatre Festival of Favorites

A five-part television series beginning June 14
Sundays at 9 PM Channel 13 PBS

Mobil

Summergarden
The Museum of Modern Art
Sculpture Garden
is open free
Fridays, Saturdays, and Sundays
6 to 10 PM
June 3 to October 2
8 West 54th Street
Made possible by a grant from Mobil

Summerpier
Free outdoor concerts
South Street Seaport Museum
Pier 16
Fulton St. and the East River
Fridays and Saturdays 8 PM
May 30 to August 31*
*Except Saturday August 9
Subway: IRT to Fulton Street IND to Broadway-Nassau Bus: M-15
Bring a blanket or chair
Made possible by a grant from Mobil
Chermayeff & Geismar

Mobil
Masterpiece
Theatre
presents
A.J. Cronin's
Doctor
Finlay
The physician
couldn't heal
himself
A six-part series
begins
Sunday, May 9
9pm on PBS
Mobil

Mobil Showcase presents

BETWEEN

THE WARS

American Diplomatic History from Versailles to Pearl Harbor
A unique 16-week television series Host: Eric Sevareid
Wednesday evenings beginning April 5 at 7:30 Channel 5

Mobil

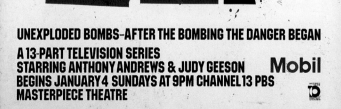

UNEXPLODED BOMBS–AFTER THE BOMBING THE DANGER BEGAN

A 13-PART TELEVISION SERIES
STARRING ANTHONY ANDREWS & JUDY GEESON
BEGINS JANUARY 4 SUNDAYS AT 9PM CHANNEL 13 PBS
MASTERPIECE THEATRE

Mobil

A dramatization of the Tolstoy novel presented on PBS-TV

Beginning November 20 Made possible by matching grants from

National Endowment for the Humanities & Mobil Oil Corporation

WAR AND PEACE

Whitney Museum
of American Art
75th & Madison
open free
Tuesday evenings

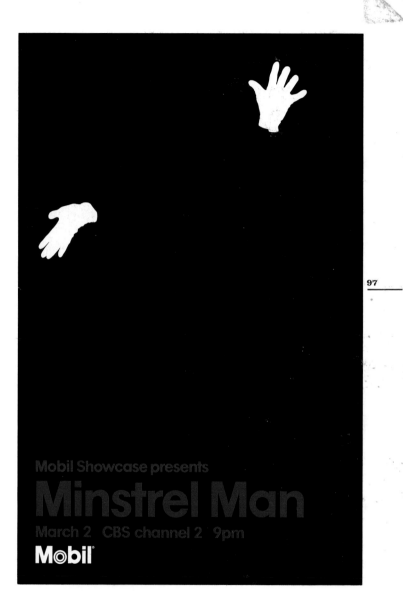
Mobil Showcase presents
Minstrel Man
March 2 CBS channel 2 9pm
Mobil

98

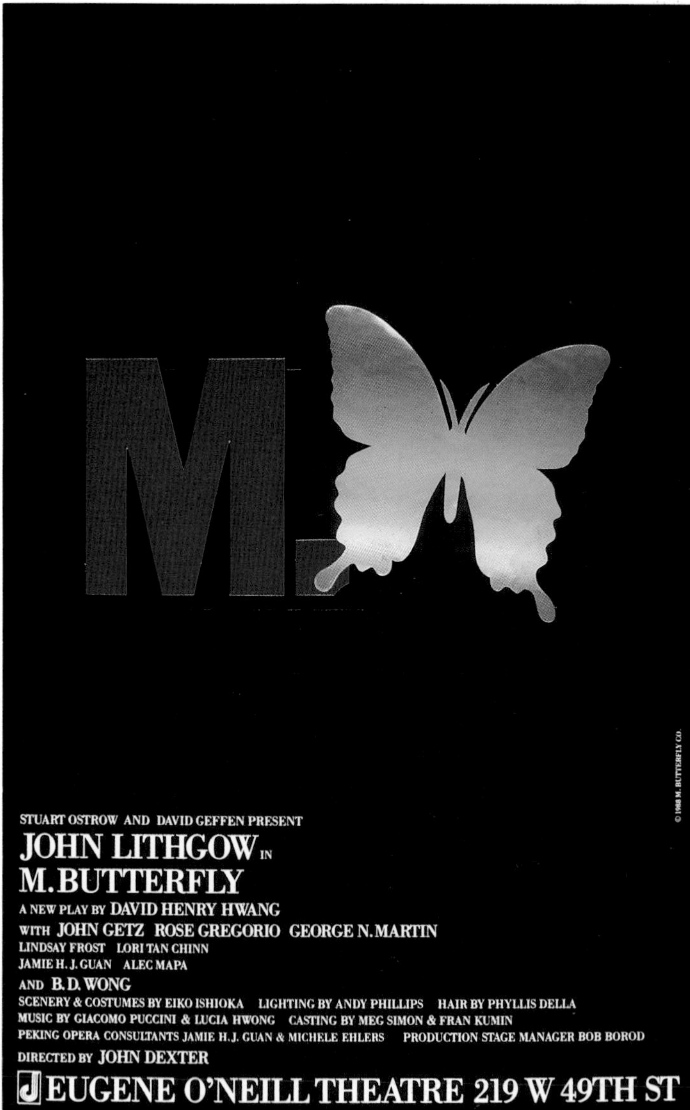
M.
STUART OSTROW AND DAVID GEFFEN PRESENT
JOHN LITHGOW IN
M. BUTTERFLY
A NEW PLAY BY DAVID HENRY HWANG
WITH JOHN GETZ ROSE GREGORIO GEORGE N. MARTIN
LINDSAY FROST LORI TAN CHINN
JAMIE H. J. GUAN ALEC MAPA
AND B. D. WONG
SCENERY & COSTUMES BY EIKO ISHIOKA LIGHTING BY ANDY PHILLIPS HAIR BY PHYLLIS DELLA
MUSIC BY GIACOMO PUCCINI & LUCIA HWONG CASTING BY MEG SIMON & FRAN KUMIN
PEKING OPERA CONSULTANTS JAMIE H.J. GUAN & MICHELE EHLERS PRODUCTION STAGE MANAGER BOB BOROD
DIRECTED BY JOHN DEXTER
EUGENE O'NEILL THEATRE 219 W 49TH ST
© 1988 M. BUTTERFLY CO.

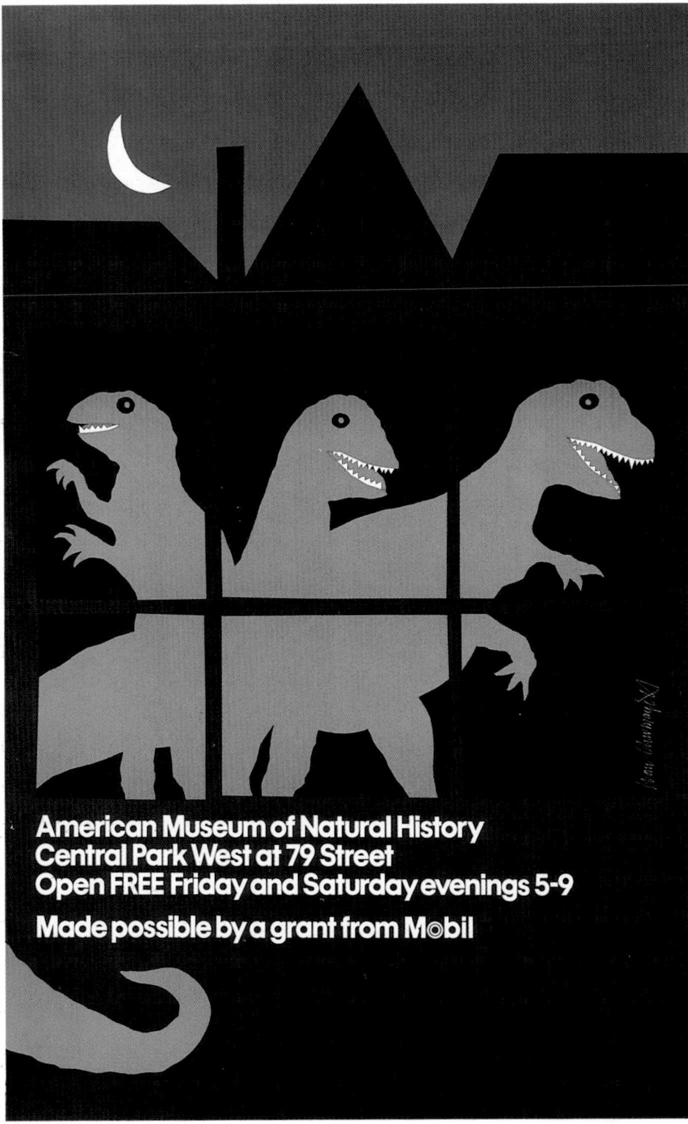
American Museum of Natural History
Central Park West at 79 Street
Open FREE Friday and Saturday evenings 5-9
Made possible by a grant from Mobil

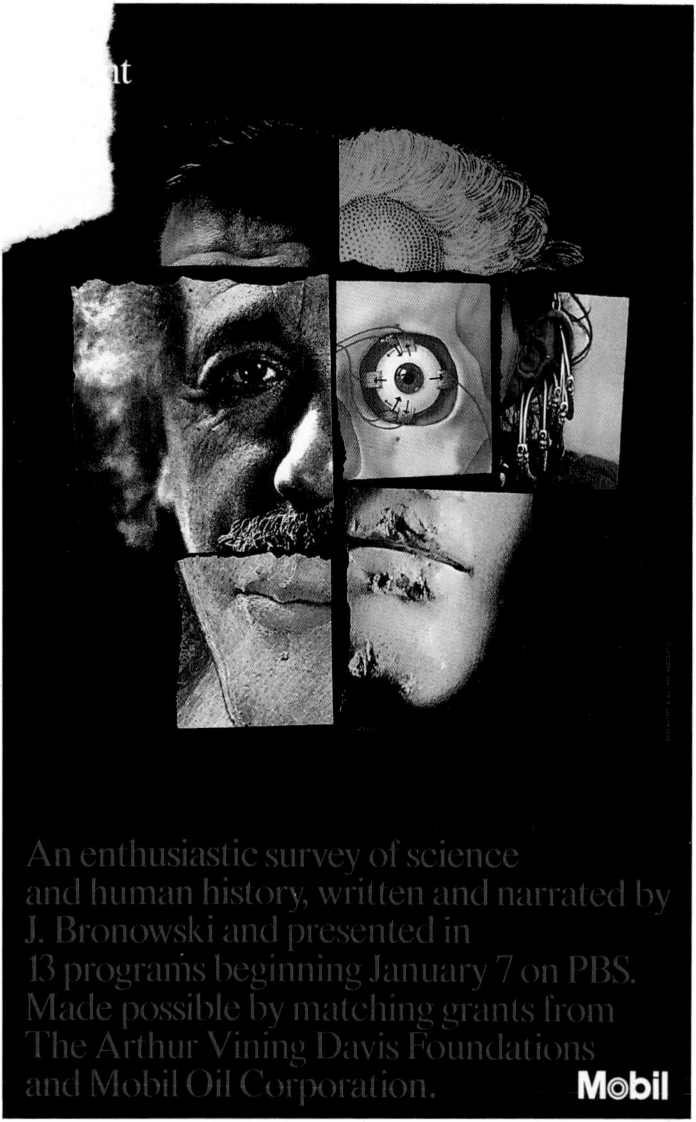
An enthusiastic survey of science
and human history, written and narrated by
J. Bronowski and presented in
13 programs beginning January 7 on PBS.
Made possible by matching grants from
The Arthur Vining Davis Foundations
and Mobil Oil Corporation.
Mobil

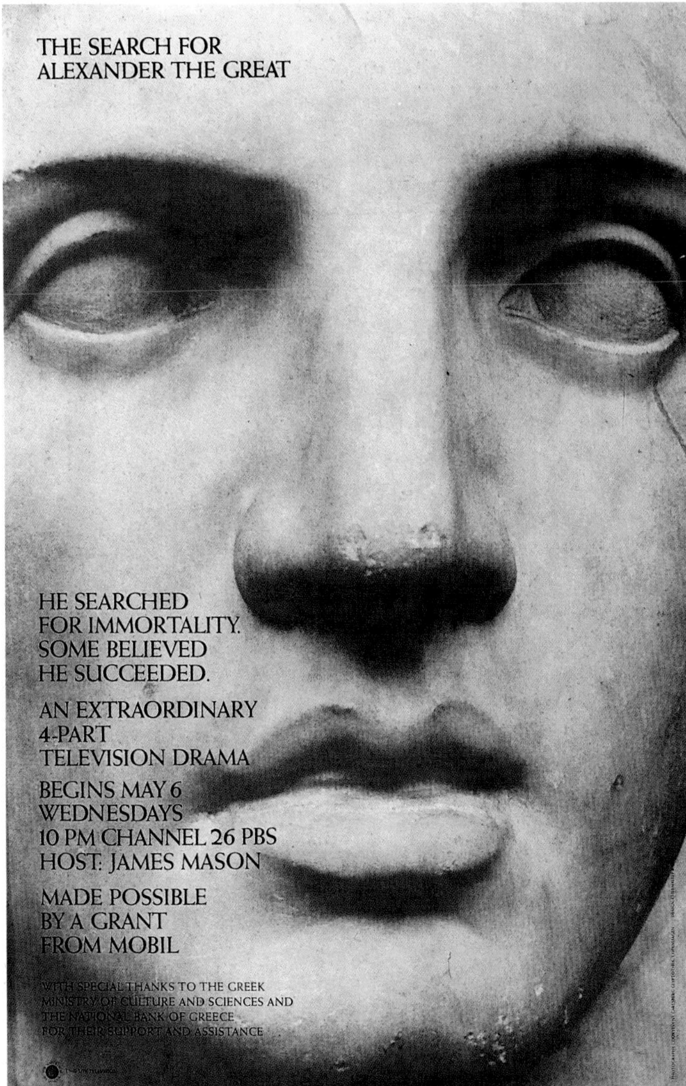
THE SEARCH FOR
ALEXANDER THE GREAT
HE SEARCHED
FOR IMMORTALITY.
SOME BELIEVED
HE SUCCEEDED.
AN EXTRAORDINARY
4-PART
TELEVISION DRAMA
BEGINS MAY 6
WEDNESDAYS
10 PM CHANNEL 26 PBS
HOST: JAMES MASON
MADE POSSIBLE
BY A GRANT
FROM MOBIL
WITH SPECIAL THANKS TO THE GREEK
MINISTRY OF CULTURE AND SCIENCES AND
THE NATIONAL BANK OF GREECE
FOR THEIR SUPPORT AND ASSISTANCE

Winston Churchill:
The Wilderness Years
He lost favor, brooded, fought and waited.
The time before his finest hour.
Starring Robert Hardy as Winston
Sian Phillips as Clementine
Mobil Masterpiece Theatre
Beginning January 16
Sundays at 9pm Channel 13 PBS
Mobil

Institute of Design 50th Anniversary

Two year celebration 1987 through 1989
Institute of Design Illinois Institute of Technology

iiT

UCLA Extension Spring Quarter begins March 28, 1992

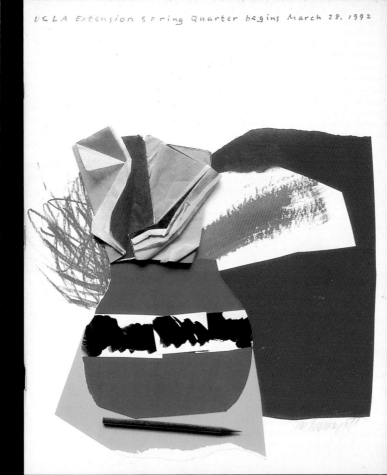

The Corcoran School of Art, Washington, D.C.

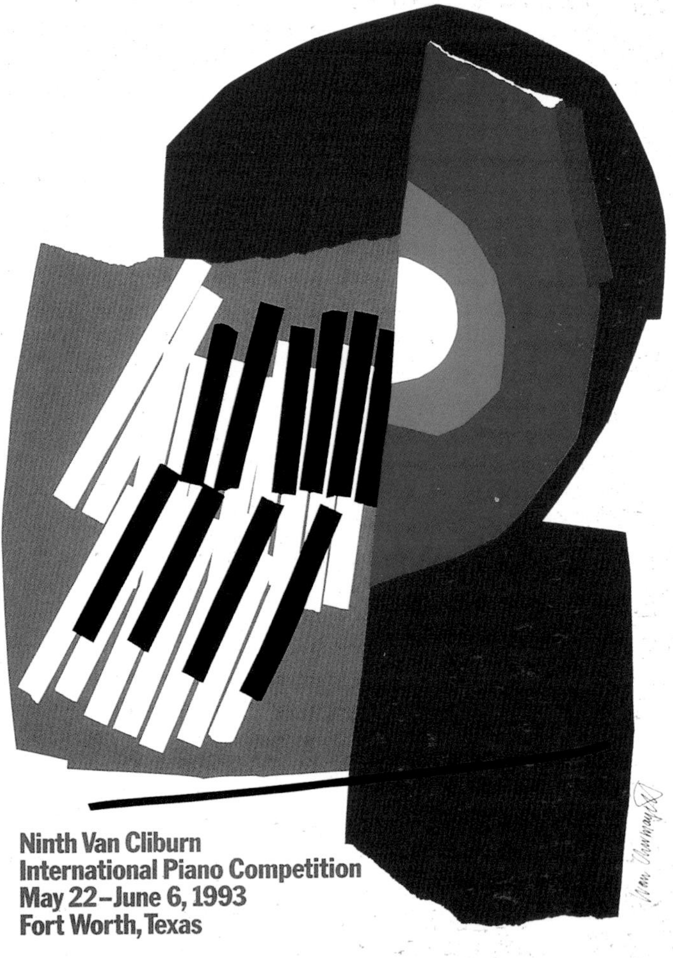
Ninth Van Cliburn
International Piano Competition
May 22–June 6, 1993
Fort Worth, Texas

The New York Times Magazine
THE SOPHISTICATED TRAVELER®
PART 2/MARCH 1, 1992
SPRING
By air
Par
437596
IMPORTANT
LISBON
TIJUANA
MIAMI

108

Ivan Chermayeff

c o l l a g e s

Jacob's**Pillow** 1990

Jacob's**Pillow** **1990**

The Spirit
of Chicago
Cocktails
Buffet
Celebrate
Join Us
Motion
Wednesday, June 12
7:00-10:00 pm
Chicago Historical Society
Clark Street at North Avenue
RSVP by June 3
The Knoll Group
212.207.2201, Laura Swift
This invitation admits or
The Knoll Group
655 Madison Avenue
New York, NY 10021

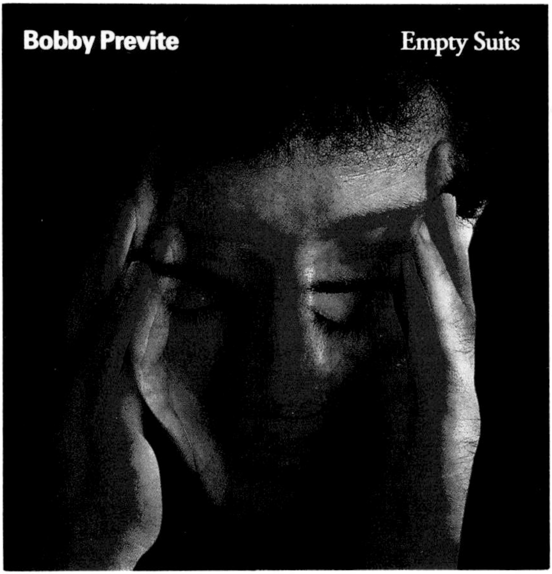

a

b

a

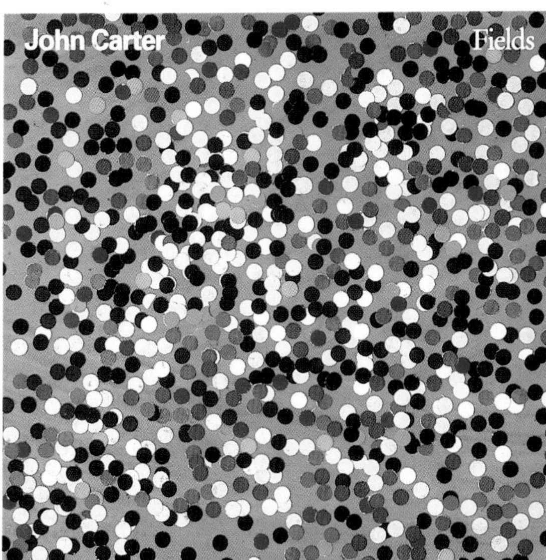

b

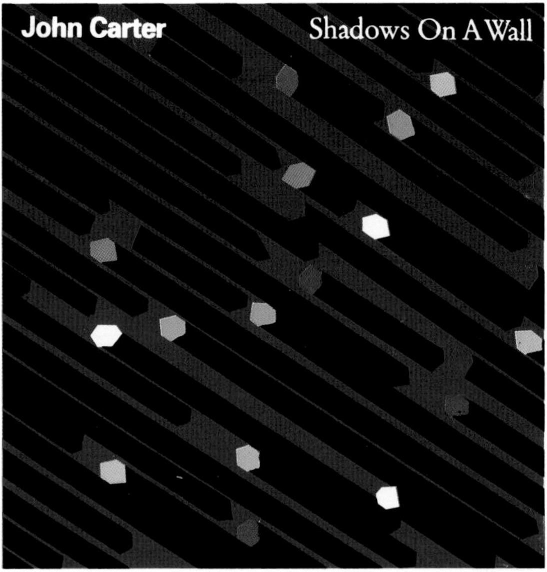

a

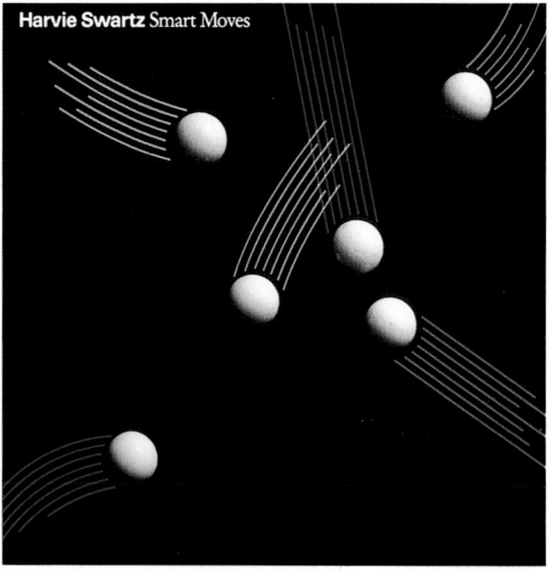

b

中央

SHOE
SHINE
SIT
DOWN
12

DEMEL, VIENNE
LES LANGUES DOREES

Ivan Chermayeff was born in 1932. He studied at Harvard University and the Institute of Design in Chicago; he graduated from Yale University. Chermayeff was a trustee of the Museum of Modern Art in New York for twenty years, and he has been a member of the Board of Directors of the International Design Conference in Aspen since 1967. In 1990, Ivan and Jane Clark Chermayeff co-chaired the 40th International Design Conference in Aspen, which was on the subject of children. He is chairman of the Educational Policy Committee of the Parsons School of Design, a trustee of the New School for Social Research and a National Trustee of the Smithsonian Institution. He is a past president of the American Institute of Graphic Art and a member of the Alliance Graphique Internationale; he has served as Andrew Carnegie Visiting Professor of Art at Cooper Union and as a visiting professor at the Kansas City Art Institute. In 1973, he was co-chairman of the First Federal Design Assembly.

AWARDS AND HONORS

In 1967, the American Institute of Architects honored Chermayeff with its Industrial Art Medal, and in 1971, the Philadelphia College of Art awarded him the Gold Medal. In 1979, Ivan Chermayeff and Thomas Geismar received the Gold Medal of the American Institute of Graphic Art. Chermayeff was named to the New York Art Directors Club Hall of Fame in 1982. In 1985, he and Thomas Geismar both received the Yale Arts Award Medal in recognition of their outstanding accomplishments in the arts. In 1991, Chermayeff received an honorary doctorate in fine arts from both the Corcoran Gallery of Art in Washington, D.C., and The University of the Arts in Philadelphia. Chermayeff has received the title Honorary Designer for Industry from the Royal Society of Arts in recognition of his achievements in graphic design.

3

MILTON glaser

MILTON GLASER

SKETCHES AND FINISHED WORKS

by MILTON GLASER

I WAS ASKED BY THE PUBLISHER OF THIS BOOK TO SHOW A SERIES OF ABOUT FIFTY WORKS. IT OCCURRED TO ME THAT A DISPLAY OF TWENTY-FIVE FINISHED PIECES ACCOMPANIED BY THEIR SKETCHES OR PRELIMINARY DRAWINGS MIGHT BE OF MORE INTEREST. FOR A VARIETY OF REASONS, DESIGNS AND ILLUSTRATIONS ARE USUALLY SEEN IN THEIR PRISTINE AND FINISHED FORM. IN THIS REGARD, THEY ARE RELATED TO A PERFORMANCE BY AN ACTOR OR MAGICIAN who has worked through the difficult details of a presentation in private in order to impress an audience with his effortlessness. If I were more of a scholar, I might be able to trace this tendency back to the beginnings of religion or to alchemy, where the means by which effects were produced were hidden from the public in order to intensify the effect.

Personally, I have always been fascinated by the prepa-

rations that proceed any finished work. When I was a child, I was lucky enough to be able to attend the rehearsals of the New York Philharmonic Orchestra, then under the direction of the great Arturo Toscanini. These were held in the old NBC Studio 8H a day before the orchestra broadcast to the world. Seeing Toscanini rework a musical phrase over and over until it matched the model he had in his mind was truly inspirational. The following afternoon, when I listened to the actual performance on the radio, I found that both my appreciation and my pleasure deepened as a consequence of witnessing the rehearsal. The sketch or rehearsal reveals the thought process of the creator in a way that a finished work is unable to do. When there are no sketches available to document creative activity, as is the case with Jan Vermeer or Piero della Francesca, for instance, we suffer a great loss.

In any event, this selection of posters and illustrations reveals my methods. In some cases, there is a direct relationship between sketch and finished work; in others, an oblique one. Occasionally there is no seeming relationship at all. What becomes obvious is that the process often reveals more than the work itself.

"NOW" OR THE PROCESS OF CHANGE IN A MOMENT

by TADANORI YOKOO, graphic designer

IN 1976, FIVE GRAPHIC DESIGNERS—ROMAN CIESLEWICZ, PAUL DAVIS, MILTON GLASER, RICHARD HESS, AND MYSELF—WERE INVITED TO SHOW THEIR WORK AT THE VENICE BIENNALE. *ESQUISSE*, OR PRELIMINARY SKETCHES, WERE EXHIBITED ALONG WITH FINISHED WORKS; THUS THE PROCESS BY WHICH EACH WORK WAS CREATED WAS MADE PUBLIC. THE FOLLOWING MILTON GLASER WORK IS DERIVED FROM THOSE CONCEPTS, BUT BY HAVING THE WORK AND THE *ESQUISSE* CONTRASTED ON OPPOSING PAGES, THE TWO ARE MADE TO BE EVEN CLOSER. SOME WORKS MAKE ONE IMAGINE THAT THERE MUST HAVE ACTUALLY BEEN MANY *ESQUISSE* DRAWN FOR EACH WORK. WE BECOME FASCINATED BY THE PROCESS OF HIS EXPRESSIONS AND THE CHANGES.

Milton Glaser's *esquisse* can also be viewed as a drawing on its own. I have often seen him sketching feverishly on a trip. I was moved by how Glaser enjoyed himself as

he made a serious drawing; yet like musicians and people in sports, he was not lax while practicing.

The results of this are very clear in the charming expressions of the *esquisse* drawings included here. What is important for creativity is not the result, but the process. A work is only complete when enough moments of "now" come together. What we experience in this book is Glaser's "now," or the process of change in a moment.

Glaser has many subjects and styles. Quotations and adaptations of elements from art history abound. I am always satisfied by his profound intellect and cultivation. The classic and the modern coexist brilliantly.

FROM POPPY WITH LOVE
MILTON GLASER

JUILLIARD

JUILLIARD
This poster, fourth in a series is made possible by a grant from TDK

JUILLIARD
This poster, third in a series is made possible by a grant from TDK

RIMINI

RIMINI
Milton Glaser

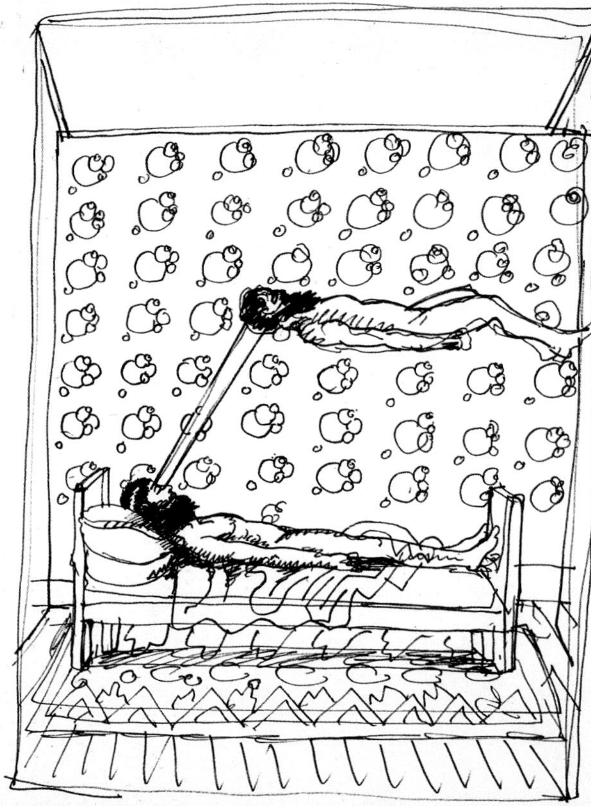

Having a talent
isn't worth much unless you know
what to do with it.
Degree and Non-Degree Programs. Day, Evening, and Saturday Sessions. Film, Photography, Media Arts (Advertising, Fashion, Illustration, Design), Crafts (Ceramics, Jewelry), Fine Arts (Painting, Sculpture, Printmaking), Video Tape, Dance, Humanities.
School of Visual Arts
209 East 23rd Street, New York, N.Y. 10010 679-7350

Milton Glaser

LAW
EQUALITY
LIBERTY
JUSTICE

AMERICAN BAR ASSOCIATION
INFORMING THE PUBLIC THROUGH EDUCATION
IN COMMEMORATION OF THE BICENTENNIAL OF THE
UNITED STATES CONSTITUTION
LAW
EQUALITY LIBERTY JUSTICE

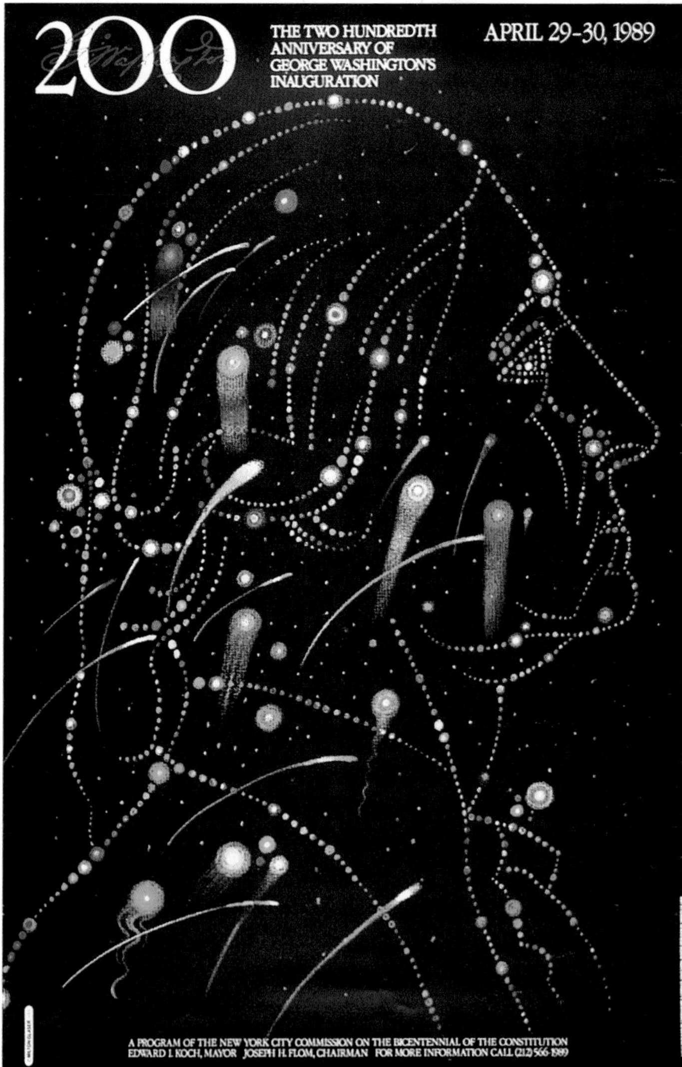
200
THE TWO HUNDREDTH
ANNIVERSARY OF
GEORGE WASHINGTON'S
INAUGURATION
APRIL 29-30, 1989
A PROGRAM OF THE NEW YORK CITY COMMISSION ON THE BICENTENNIAL OF THE CONSTITUTION
EDWARD I. KOCH, MAYOR JOSEPH H. FLOM, CHAIRMAN FOR MORE INFORMATION CALL (212) 566-1989

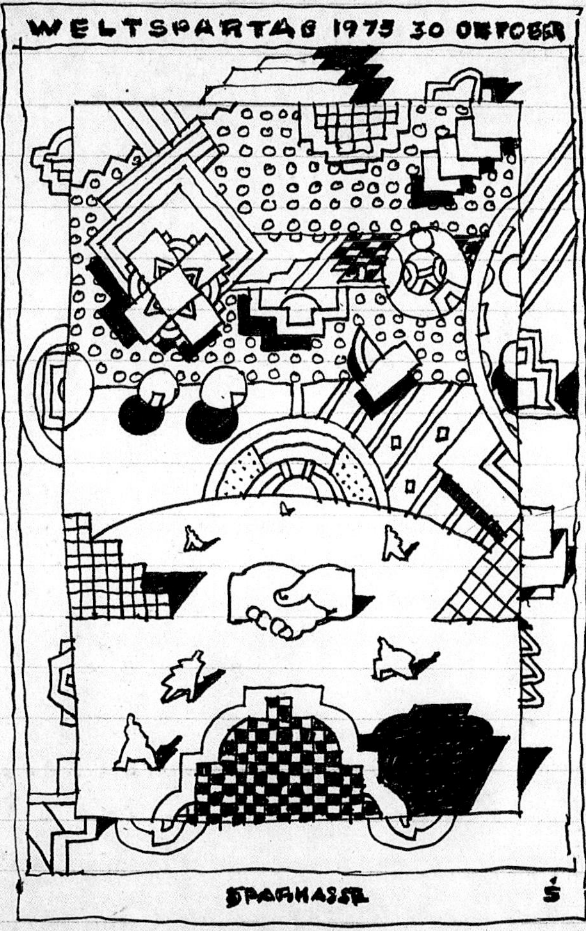
WELTSPARTAG 1975 30 OKTOBER
SPARKASSE

S E V I L L A
EXPO'92

152

CENTER FOR THE PERFORMING ARTS AT BROOKLYN COLLEGE
CELEBRATING
THE
PERFORMING
ARTS AT
BROOKLYN
COLLEGE
35TH ANNIVERSARY FESTIVAL-FEB.28 TO MAR.11,1990

SAN FRANCISCO OPERA
Kurt Herbert Adler, General Director
59TH SEASON
1981

20TH ANNIVERSARY 1974/1994
A PROMISE KEPT
MIDDLE COLLEGE HIGH SCHOOL
At LaGuardia Community College/CUNY

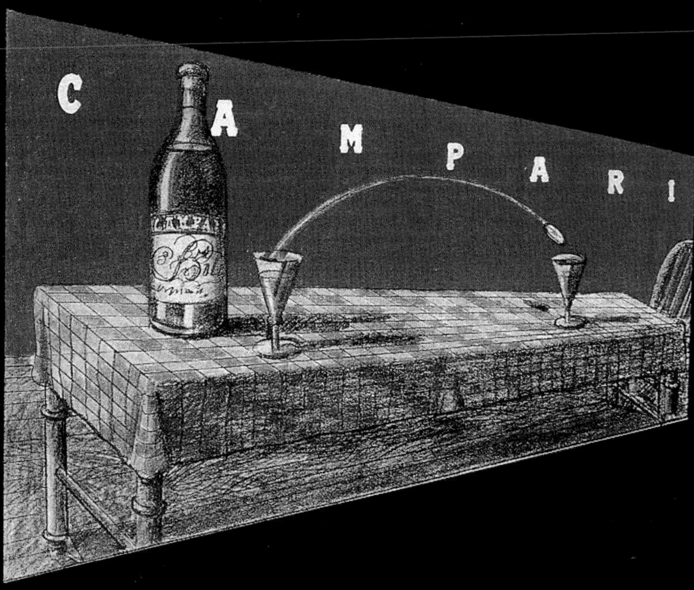
C A M P A R I

CAMPARI
Bitter

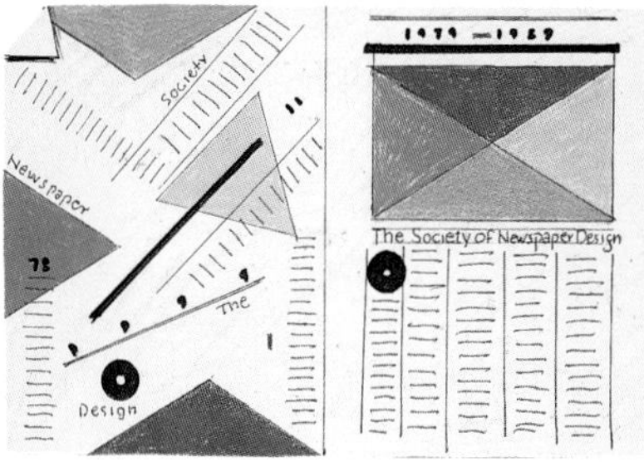
Society
Newspaper
The
Design
The Society of Newspaper Design

Society
Newspaper
1989
Design
MILTON GLASER

1979 — 1989
The Society of Newspaper Design
of
PHOTOGRAPH BY MATTHEW KLEIN

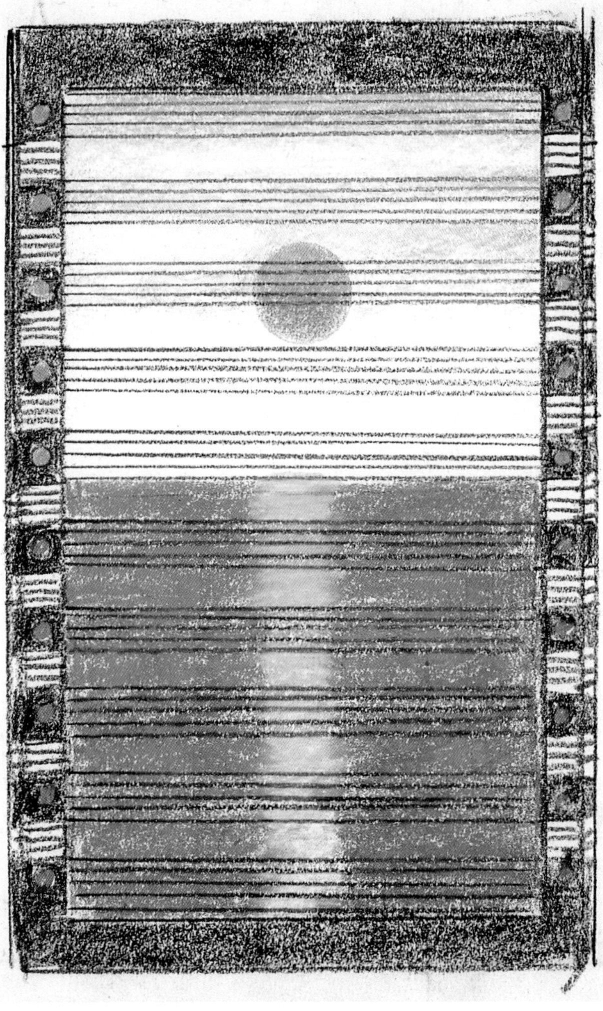

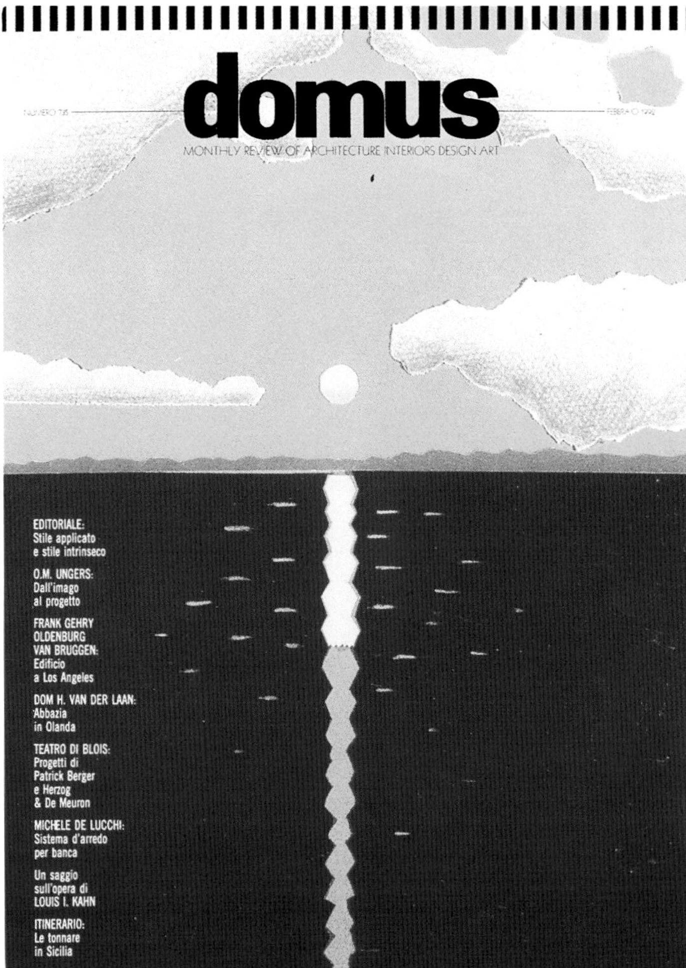
domus
MONTHLY REVIEW OF ARCHITECTURE INTERIORS DESIGN ART
EDITORIALE:
Stile applicato
e stile intrinseco
O.M. UNGERS:
Dall'imago
al progetto
FRANK GEHRY
OLDENBURG
VAN BRUGGEN:
Edificio
a Los Angeles
DOM H. VAN DER LAAN:
Abbazia
in Olanda
TEATRO DI BLOIS:
Progetti di
Patrick Berger
e Herzog
& De Meuron
MICHELE DE LUCCHI:
Sistema d'arredo
per banca
Un saggio
sull'opera di
LOUIS I. KAHN
ITINERARIO:
Le tonnare
in Sicilia

Print

$10
AMERICA'S GRAPHIC DESIGN MAGAZINE
NOVEMBER/DECEMBER 1993
PRINT XLVII:VI
Print
THE ITALIAN ISSUE
Milton Glaser

165

Studies for Gogol – [illegible]

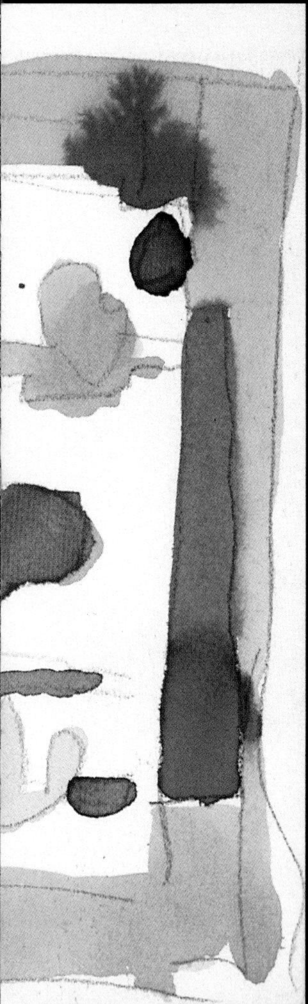

2
CALL FOR ENTRIES
SECOND
INTERNATIONAL
EXHIBITION
NEW YORK NY
MAY 1988

DEADLINE: 4 DECEMBER 1987
The Art Directors Club, Inc.
SECOND INTERNATIONAL EXHIBITION
CALL FOR ENTRIES
NEW YORK, NY 10003 U.S.A.
The Art Directors Club of New York is extending its prestigious annual awards program to the international design and advertising community. The 2nd International Exhibition, a juried competition for excellence in print, television and film art direction, will be judged by a distinguished panel of ADC Hall of Fame laureates and designers of international stature.

The Many lights of Aurora

New
Old

Words
In words as fashions the same rule will hold.
Alike fantastic if too new or old.
Be not the first by whom the new are tried.
Nor yet the last to lay the old aside.
Alexander Pope
Image
OLD
NEW
Thoughts
OLD
OLD
School of Visual Arts
A COLLEGE OF THE ARTS
B.F.A. Programs in Advertising, Animation, Art Education,
Art Therapy, Cartooning, Computer Art, Film and Video, Fine Arts,
Graphic Design, Illustration, Interior Design, Photography
M.F.A. Programs in Computer Art, Fine Arts, Illustration, Photography
and Continuing Education Programs
209 E. 23 ST., N.Y.C., 10010-3994 1-800-366-7820 FAX: 212-725-3587

DESIGN
TALK
Design
Talk
DESIGN
TALK

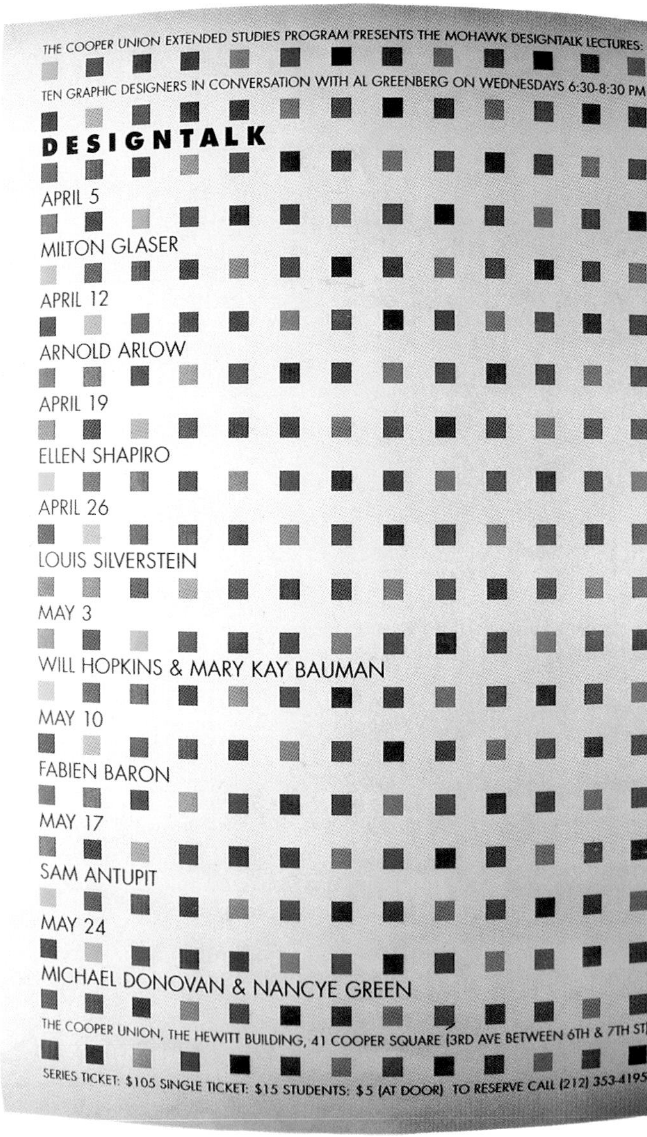
THE COOPER UNION EXTENDED STUDIES PROGRAM PRESENTS THE MOHAWK DESIGNTALK LECTURES:
TEN GRAPHIC DESIGNERS IN CONVERSATION WITH AL GREENBERG ON WEDNESDAYS 6:30-8:30 PM
DESIGNTALK
APRIL 5
MILTON GLASER
APRIL 12
ARNOLD ARLOW
APRIL 19
ELLEN SHAPIRO
APRIL 26
LOUIS SILVERSTEIN
MAY 3
WILL HOPKINS & MARY KAY BAUMAN
MAY 10
FABIEN BARON
MAY 17
SAM ANTUPIT
MAY 24
MICHAEL DONOVAN & NANCYE GREEN
THE COOPER UNION, THE HEWITT BUILDING, 41 COOPER SQUARE (3RD AVE BETWEEN 6TH & 7TH ST)
SERIES TICKET: $105 SINGLE TICKET: $15 STUDENTS: $5 (AT DOOR) TO RESERVE CALL (212) 353-4195

WOLF TRAP
THIS POSTER MADE POSSIBLE BY A GRANT FROM NORTHERN TELECOM INC.

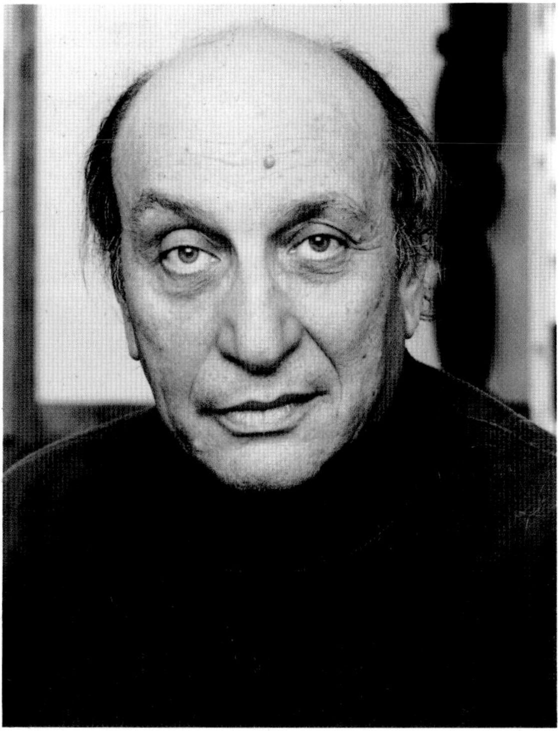

Photo by Stephen Green-Armytage

Born in New York City in 1929, Milton Glaser was educated at the High School of Music and Art, New York (1943–46); at The Cooper Union Art School, New York (1948–51); and, via Fulbright Scholarship, at the Academy of Fine Arts, Bologna, Italy (1952–53). In 1954, along with Reynold Ruffins, Seymour Chwast, and Edward Sorel, he was founder and president of Push Pin Studios, New York. In 1968, he and Clay Felker founded New York Magazine. In 1983, Glaser teamed with Walter Bernard to form WBMG, a publication design firm located in New York.

Glaser's graphic and architectural commissions include the I Love NY logo (1976); the redesign of the identity of a principal American supermarket chain for the Grand Union Company (including architectural, interior, packaging, and advertising design); the redevelopment of the Rainbow Room complexes for the Rockefeller Center Management Corporation (1987); the overall conceptualization and interior design of New York Unearthed, a museum located in Manhattan's South Street Seaport (1990); and the logo for Tony Kushner's Pulitzer Prize-winning play ANGELS IN AMERICA (1993).

Glaser is also personally responsible for the design and illustration of over three hundred posters for clients in the areas of publishing, music, theater, and film, as well as those for commercial products and services.

Glaser's artwork has been exhibited worldwide. The following exhibitions are most notable: a one-man show at the Museum of Modern Art, New York (1975); the Centre Georges Pompidou, Paris (1977); a one-man show at the Vicenza Museum, Italy (1989); "Giorgio Morandi/Milton Glaser," at the Galleria Communale d'Arte Moderna, Italy (1989); "Piero della Francesca" Arezzo, Italy (1991), Milan, Italy (1992); "The Imaginary Life of Claude Monet," Nuages Gallery, Italy (1994); and the Creation Gallery G8, Japan (1995). His work is held in the permanent collections at the Museum of Modern Art, New York; The Israel Museum, Jerusalem; and the National Archive, Smithsonian Institution, Washington, D.C.

4

PAUL rand

PAUL RAND

by YUSAKU KAMEKURA, graphic designer

THE FIRST TIME I VISITED PAUL RAND AT HIS HOME WAS IN THE FALL OF 1954. NEEDLESS TO SAY, WE WERE BOTH STILL QUITE YOUNG BACK IN THOSE DAYS. YET EVEN THEN THE NAME PAUL RAND WAS ALREADY WIDELY KNOWN, AND WIDELY ACCLAIMED, THROUGHOUT THE ENTIRE WORLD.

In my mind, the word that probably fit Paul Rand best is "genius." His extraordinary talents were confirmed early on by his selection to serve as art director of one of America's leading magazines, *Esquire*, at the tender age of twenty-three. As his remarkable talents continued to develop and mature in the years after our first meeting, he energetically proceeded to produce a succession of exceptional works that clearly mirrored the depth of his intellectual powers. He swept up nearly every prize—and wide renown—as a result.

Looking back over the course of Paul Rand's artistic

career, one is inevitably moved by the abundance of lyrical beauty in his works and by their diverse expressive methods, which were infallibly matched to their times. What attracts us most in his works are their concise expression, their superfluity cast aside, their bright and cheerful colors, and their powerful and solid design sense. Yet perhaps most important to his works' appeal is the fact that Paul Rand himself was a born poet.

Paul Rand is often said to have been one of the greatest, and most "American," of America's artists. The notion no doubt arose from his explicit straightness and spirited brilliance—artistic sensibilities inevitably born from an environment shaped by freedom. His urbane and stylish ideas, his sophisticated messages, and his bright and witty humor all symbolized the essence of American culture. And yet, symbol of America though he is, Paul Rand was, one should remember, a man of profound intellectual and philosophical depth. He was especially enamored of Eastern philosophy, and on occasion I detect very Japanese feelings in his works. I'm not referring to mere exoticism with a Japanese bent. What I see is something much deeper and more spiritual. Indeed, his forms are often more "Japanese" than those of most Japanese artists. In the years after World War II, we Japanese rushed, and writhed, to catch up with Western culture. Our struggle to absorb as much of the West as possible was, in some ways, touchingly sad; yet we believed that

this was our only means of surviving. In our haste, we all too often considered Japanese traditions as a hindrance. Today, thinking back on the pressures we felt in those times, the situation seems rather heartrending.

When we Japanese look at Paul Rand's works and ponder the futility of our struggle to absorb Western culture, we are stunned to recognize traditional Japanese styles—styles which we Japanese have long forgotten—running beautifully and refreshingly through them. Even more importantly, in his every work we marvel at the wondrous vitality we find there that transcends all notions of time.

The
graphic art
of Paul Rand

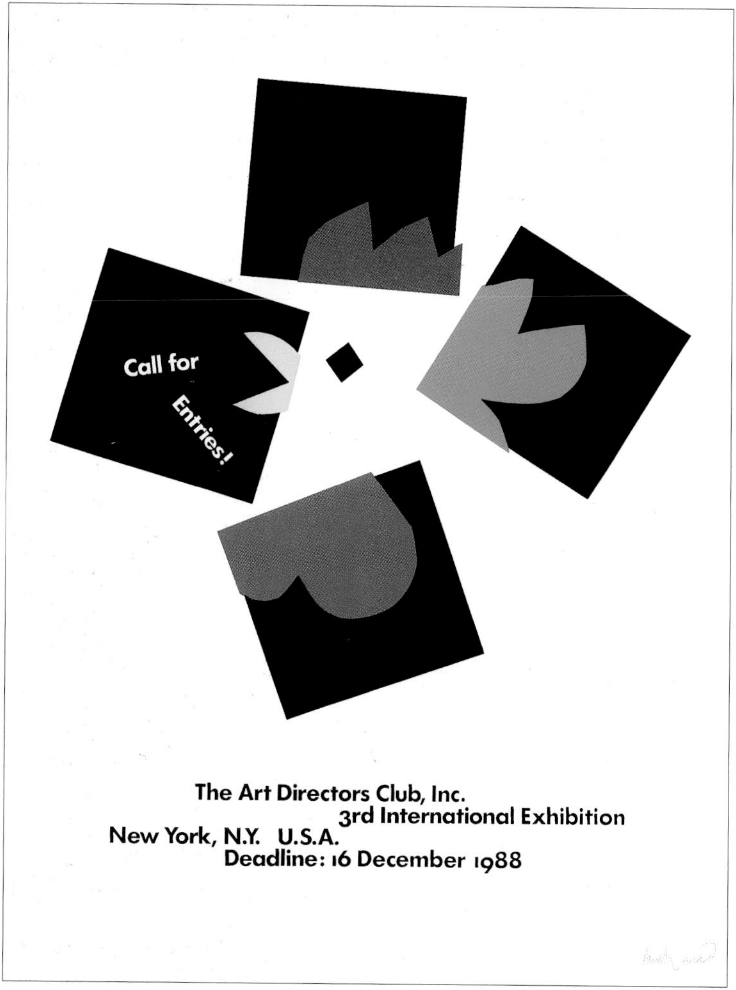
Call for
Entries!
The Art Directors Club, Inc.
3rd International Exhibition
New York, N.Y. U.S.A.
Deadline: 16 December 1988

DADA

A Keepsake of Advertising Typographers Association of America
with the sense of sight,
the idea communicates the emotion...
Alfred North Whitehead

193

The Prepared Professional
International Design Conference in Aspen
June 13–18, '82
As modern society moves from the earlier dominance of agriculture and industry into its tertiary or cybernetic phase, the role of the professional becomes central.
Old questions take on new meanings.
How is the professional prepared?
What, in a fast-changing scene, should he prepare for?
How do roles and responsibilities change?
What happens to the traditional values of the professional?
How does he adapt to the pressures of a mass society?
What kind of future does he look forward to?
Registration Fees: (U.S. Dollars) $300; One Additional Member of Household
List all applicants by name and make check payable to IDCA and mail with registration to: IDCA c/o The Bank of Aspen, P.O. Box O, Aspen, Colorado 81612 (Your cancelled check is your confirmation.)
Housing and Travel: Aspen Ski Tours, 300 South Spring Street, Aspen, Colorado 81611 (303 925 4526) and/or Aspen Central Reservations, 700 South Aspen Street, Aspen, Colorado 81611 (303 925 9000)
Camping information: U.S. Forest Service, 806 West Hallum, Aspen, Colorado 81611
Additional information: IDCA, P.O. Box 664, Aspen, Colorado 81612 (303 925 2257 or 303 925 6265)

NeXT
The sign of
the NeXT generation
of computers...
for Education

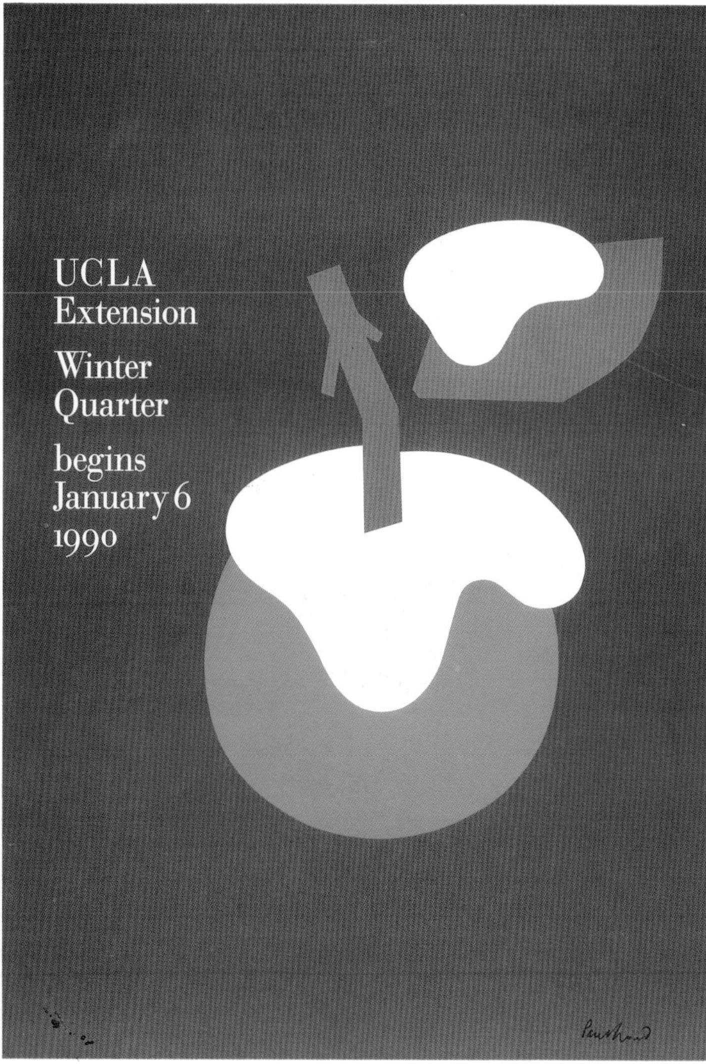
UCLA
Extension
Winter
Quarter
begins
January 6
1990

Tokyo
Communication
Arts
Osaka
Communication
Arts
Paul Rand

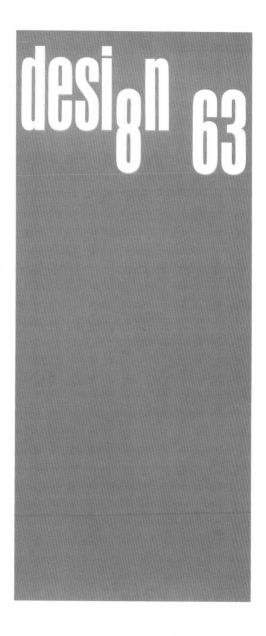
desi8n 63

RM
Resource Management:
Energy and
Materials Conservation
Ridesharing
Environment Protection

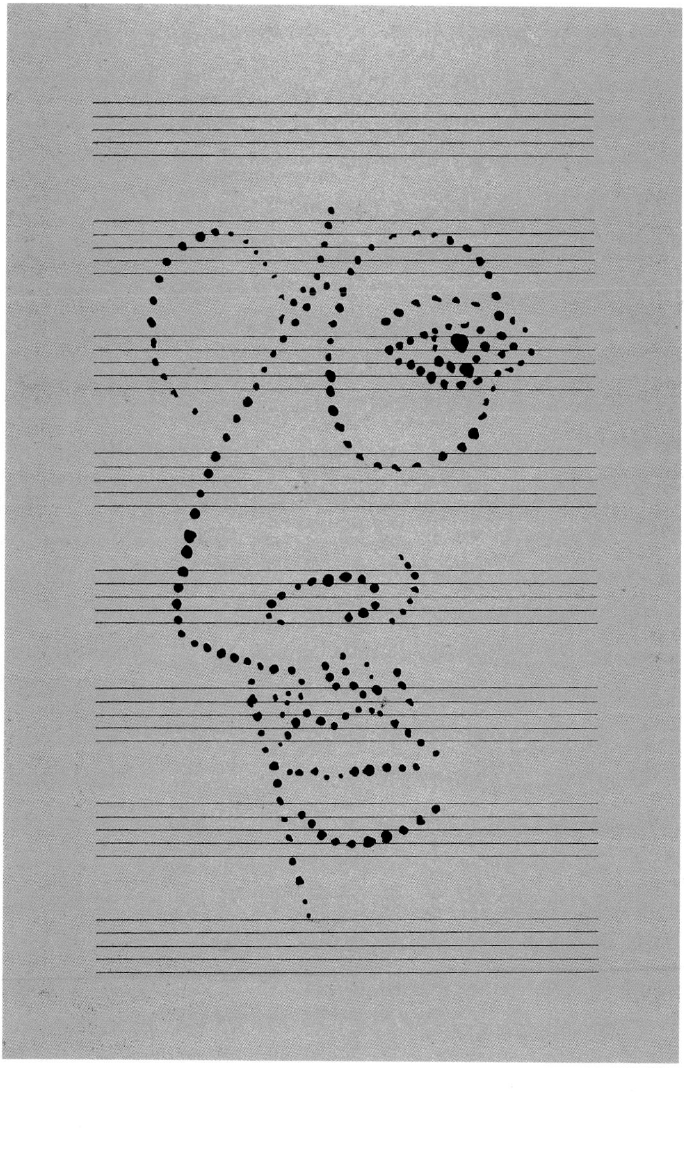

Paul Rand '68

IBM
New Methods for Knowing

9

The 13-line logo was designed to accommodate those requirements calling for a more restrained visual interpretation, e.g. legal documents, certificates, etc. Technical problems like printing, embossing, die cutting, and engraving largely determine whether or not the 8-line or 13-line logo should be used.

For most applications, however, the 8-line is preferable. If a more discreet visual effect is needed, it may be grayed down to approximate the tonal value of the 13-line logo.

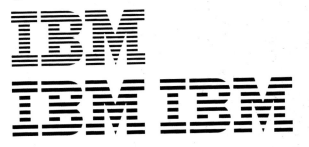

The concept of quality is difficult to define, for it is not merely seen, but somehow intuited in the presence of the work in which it is embodied.

Quality has little to do with popular notions of beauty, taste, or style; and nothing to do with status, respectability, or luxury. It is revealed, rather, in an atmosphere of receptivity, propriety, and restraint. Paul Rand

IBM

PDR
Pastore DePamphilis Rampone
New Headquarters:
303 Park Avenue South
New York, NY 10010
212 477 3300
Computer Typography
Printing
Halftone Reproductions
Color Transfers
Printing: PDR Halftone Reproductions

A

B

C

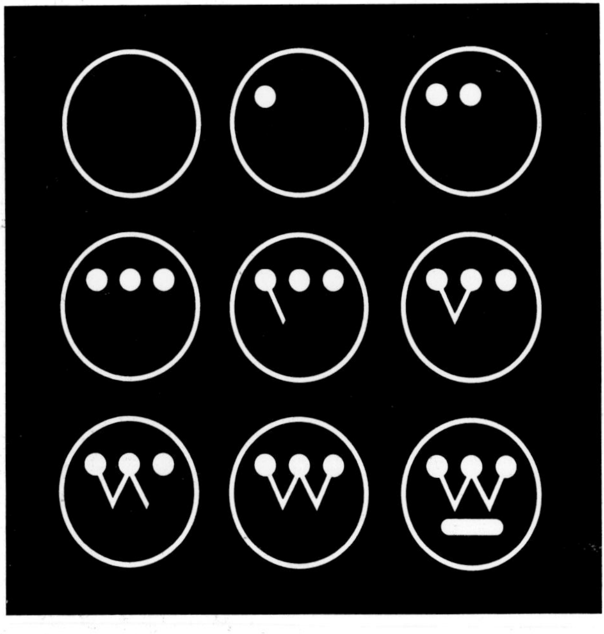

ups

Things
we know about
tomorrow:
10,000
Traffic Signals
Controlled
by a Computer...
Imagine a computer that could solve the downtown traffic problem. This is the long-range potential of a new kind of computer invented by Westinghouse, one that could control ten thousand traffic signals, and move more cars with fewer delays. This computer "learns" by experience, tries new approaches when necessary, adapts instantly to changing problems. Right now it's at work in industry. One pilot model has been running a refinery process, not to produce the greatest number of tons, not to produce the highest profit per ton, but to produce the highest total profit for the equipment. This new-concept computer will improve the making of cement, paper, and almost anything else made by a continuous process. Compared to standard computers, the new type will be smaller, simpler, more reliable. You can be sure...if it's
Westinghouse
Paul Rand

To Catch a Hummingbird
How the Gemini Spacecraft will find its target . . .
Suppose you had to capture alive one little hummingbird flying a known course high over the Amazon jungle. Difficult? Sure, but no more so than the job assigned to a new radar system Westinghouse is building for the NASA-Gemini space program.
The bird is an Agena rocket, orbiting the earth at 17,500 miles per hour. The hunter, in an intersecting orbit, is the Gemini two-man spacecraft being built by McDonnell Aircraft.
And so the hunt begins. The spacecraft radar finds the target and starts an electronic question-and-answer game.
A computer keeps score, giving the astronauts continuous readings on angles and approach speeds until the vehicles are joined. The hummingbird is caught.
The Gemini experiments will be a prelude to the first moon trip. And Westinghouse is already working on advanced radar systems for lunar landings and deep space missions.
You can be sure . . . if it's Westinghouse.
We never forget how much you rely on Westinghouse.
Westinghouse

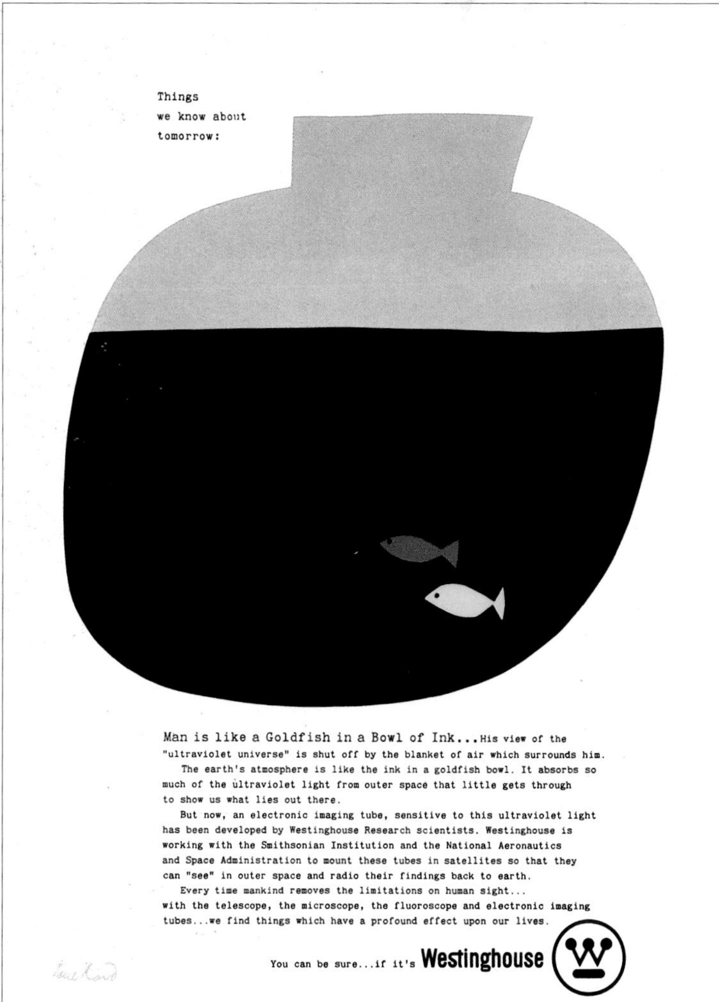
Things
we know about
tomorrow:
Man is like a Goldfish in a Bowl of Ink...His view of the "ultraviolet universe" is shut off by the blanket of air which surrounds him.
The earth's atmosphere is like the ink in a goldfish bowl. It absorbs so much of the ultraviolet light from outer space that little gets through to show us what lies out there.
But now, an electronic imaging tube, sensitive to this ultraviolet light has been developed by Westinghouse Research scientists. Westinghouse is working with the Smithsonian Institution and the National Aeronautics and Space Administration to mount these tubes in satellites so that they can "see" in outer space and radio their findings back to earth.
Every time mankind removes the limitations on human sight... with the telescope, the microscope, the fluoroscope and electronic imaging tubes...we find things which have a profound effect upon our lives.
You can be sure...if it's Westinghouse

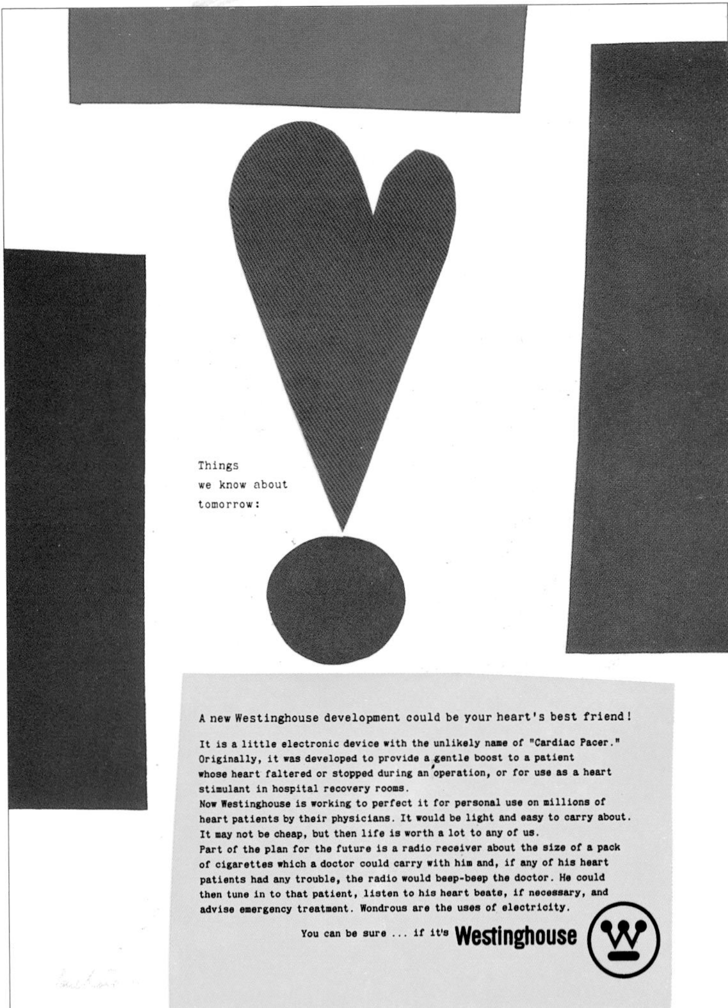
Things
we know about
tomorrow:
A new Westinghouse development could be your heart's best friend!
It is a little electronic device with the unlikely name of "Cardiac Pacer." Originally, it was developed to provide a gentle boost to a patient whose heart faltered or stopped during an operation, or for use as a heart stimulant in hospital recovery rooms.
Now Westinghouse is working to perfect it for personal use on millions of heart patients by their physicians. It would be light and easy to carry about. It may not be cheap, but then life is worth a lot to any of us.
Part of the plan for the future is a radio receiver about the size of a pack of cigarettes which a doctor could carry with him and, if any of his heart patients had any trouble, the radio would beep-beep the doctor. He could then tune in to that patient, listen to his heart beats, if necessary, and advise emergency treatment. Wondrous are the uses of electricity.
You can be sure ... if it's Westinghouse

218

City of Westminster
GERRARD PLACE W.
LAURENCE OLIVIER PRODUCTIONS
ST. JAMES'S THEATRE
GARRICK THEATRE
JOHN MILLS
TOP OF THE LADDER
Written and Produced by TYRONE GUTHRIE
DIANA WYNYARD
JAMES DONALD
"CAPTAIN CARVALLO"
New Comedy by DENIS CANNAN
TOUCH and GO
Revue FROM PARIS
Darryl F. Zanuck
presents: Richard Widmark
Linda Darnell
Stephen McNally
no
with - Sidney Poitier, Mildred Joanne Smith, Harry Bellaver,
JOAN FONTAINE JOSEPH COTTEN
FRANCOISE ROSAY
HAL WALLIS
"September Affair"
PLAZA

out
Johnson
written by Joseph L. Mankiewicz
and Lesser Samuels
produced by Darryl F. Zanuck... directed by Joseph L. Mankiewicz
TOUGH AS NAILS DRAMA
OF THE BIG HOUSE!
GLENN
BRODERICK
FORD-CRAWFORD
CONVICTED
PLAZA
September Affair
PLAZA
September Affair
PLAZA

220

CORONET
makes the lighter highball
...because Coronet itself
is lighter...kinder...
cleaner-tasting!
lighter with soda...
lighter with ginger ale...
lighter with cola...
VSQ
CORONET
VSQ
Fine Brandy
CORONET BRANDY
Paul Rand

Dubonnet
made to order
for
summer!
DUBONNET
Dubonnet
An Aperitif Wine
MADE SINCE 1846
Dubonnet PARTY PUNCH
Pour 1 bottle Dubonnet into pitcher. Add 1 pint gin. Add juice of 6 limes and shells, large bottle of soda. Stir. Serve with ice in tall glasses.
For your summer parties, remember this...no drink turns off the heat like a frosty Dubonnet cooler. Dubonnet is so mild, it always treats you like the gentleman you are! It's the nicest way known to make an occasion out of a meal. Try Dubonnet tonight!
For free recipe book (in states where legal) write Dept. B, Dubonnet Corp., Phila., Pa.
Dubonnet Aperitif Wine, Product of U.S.A. © 1954 Dubonnet Corp., Phila., Pa.
MERRY WIDOW
One-half Dubonnet. One-half dry vermouth. Stir with ice. Strain. Add twist of lemon peel.
Dubonnet LIME RICKEY
1½ jiggers of Dubonnet. Juice of half a lime, with shell. Add ice cubes, soda and stir.
Dubonnet COCKTAIL
One-half Dubonnet. One-half gin. Stir with ice. Strain. Add twist of lemon peel.
Dubonnet ON-THE-ROCKS
Pour over ice cubes. Add twist of lemon peel.
Dubonnet and soda
jigger of Dubonnet
juice of ¼ lemon
add ice cubes
fill with soda and stir.
Dubonnet STRAIGHT
Serve well chilled, no ice. Add twist of lemon peel.

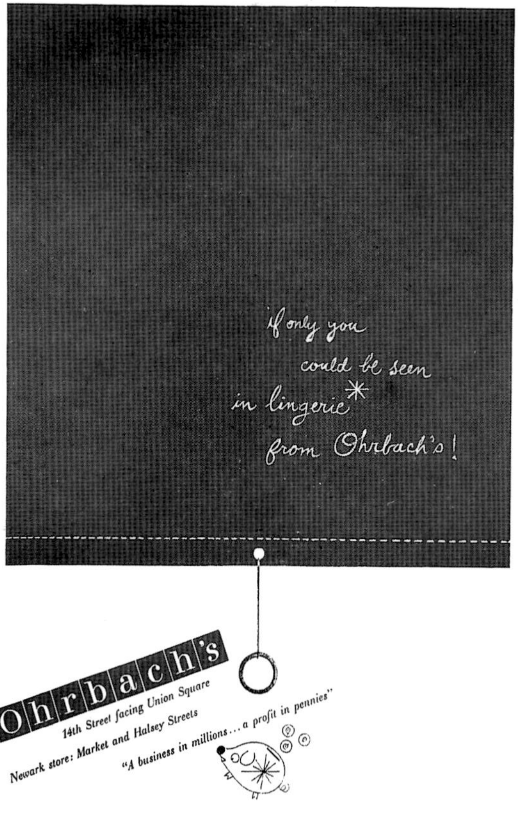
If only you
could be seen
in lingerie*
from Ohrbach's!
Ohrbach's
14th Street facing Union Square
Newark store: Market and Halsey Streets
"A business in millions... a profit in pennies"

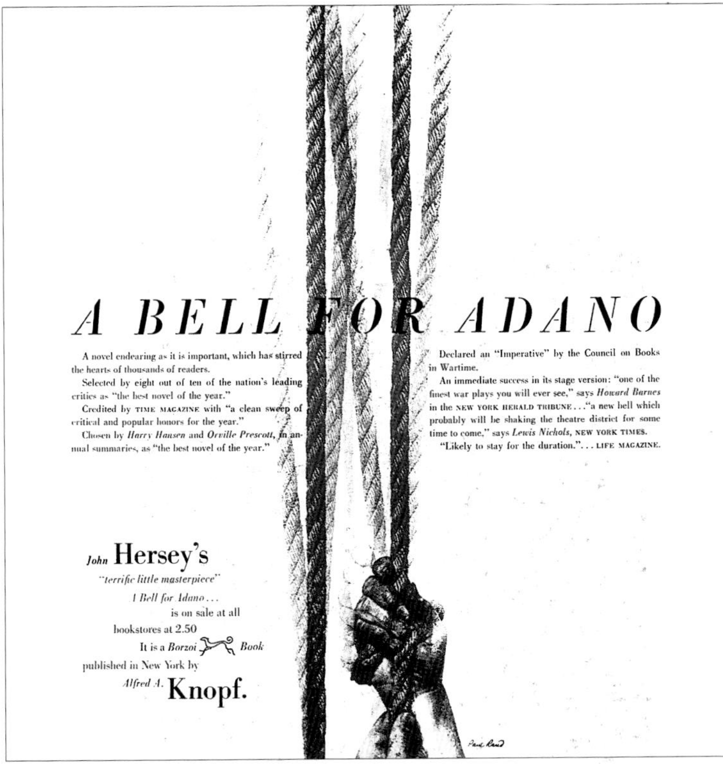
A BELL FOR ADANO
A novel endearing as it is important, which has stirred the hearts of thousands of readers.
Selected by eight out of ten of the nation's leading critics as "the best novel of the year."
Credited by TIME MAGAZINE with "a clean sweep of critical and popular honors for the year."
Chosen by Harry Hansen and Orville Prescott, in annual summaries, as "the best novel of the year."
Declared an "Imperative" by the Council on Books in Wartime.
An immediate success in its stage version: "one of the finest war plays you will ever see," says Howard Barnes in the NEW YORK HERALD TRIBUNE..."a new bell which probably will be shaking the theatre district for some time to come," says Lewis Nichols, NEW YORK TIMES.
"Likely to stay for the duration."... LIFE MAGAZINE.
John Hersey's
"terrific little masterpiece"
A Bell for Adano...
is on sale at all
bookstores at 2.50
It is a Borzoi Book
published in New York by
Alfred A. Knopf.
Paul Rand

To the executives and management of the Radio Corporation of America:

Messrs. Alexander, Anderson, Baker, Buck, Cahill, Cannon, Carter, Coe, Coffin, Dunlap, Elliott, Engstrom, Folsom, Gorin, Jolliffe, Kayes, Marek, Mills, Odorizzi, Orth, Sacks, Brig. Gen. Sarnoff, R. Sarnoff, Saxon, Seidel, Teegarden, Tuft, Watts, Weaver, Werner, Williams

Gentlemen: An important message intended expressly for your eyes is now on its way to each one of you by special messenger.

William H. Weintraub & Company, Inc. *Advertising* *488 Madison Avenue, New York*

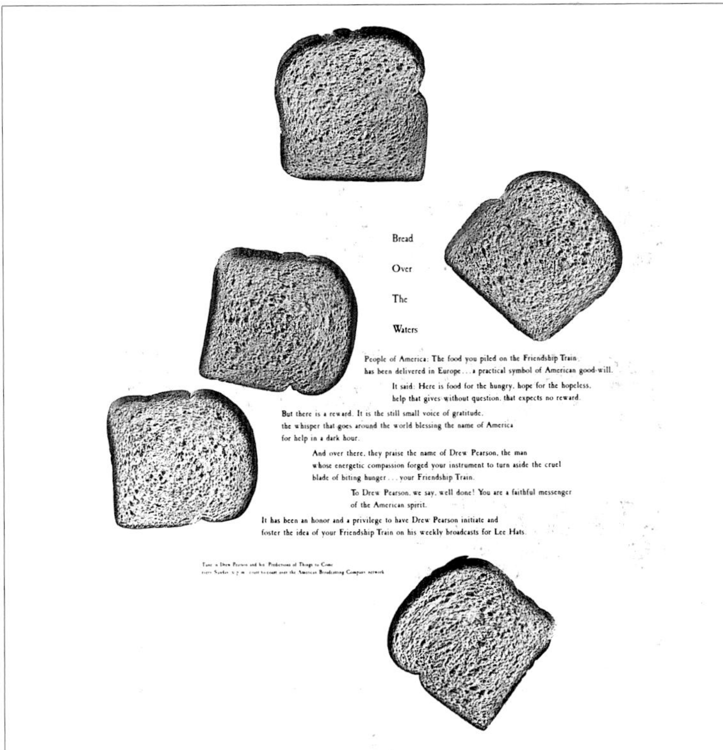
Bread
Over
The
Waters
People of America: The food you piled on the Friendship Train has been delivered in Europe . . . a practical symbol of American good-will.
It said: Here is food for the hungry, hope for the hopeless, help that gives without question, that expects no reward.
But there is a reward. It is the still small voice of gratitude, the whisper that goes around the world blessing the name of America for help in a dark hour.
And over there, they praise the name of Drew Pearson, the man whose energetic compassion forged your instrument to turn aside the cruel blade of biting hunger . . . your Friendship Train.
To Drew Pearson, we say, well done! You are a faithful messenger of the American spirit.
It has been an honor and a privilege to have Drew Pearson initiate and foster the idea of your Friendship Train on his weekly broadcasts for Lee Hats.
Tune in Drew Pearson and his Predictions of Things to Come

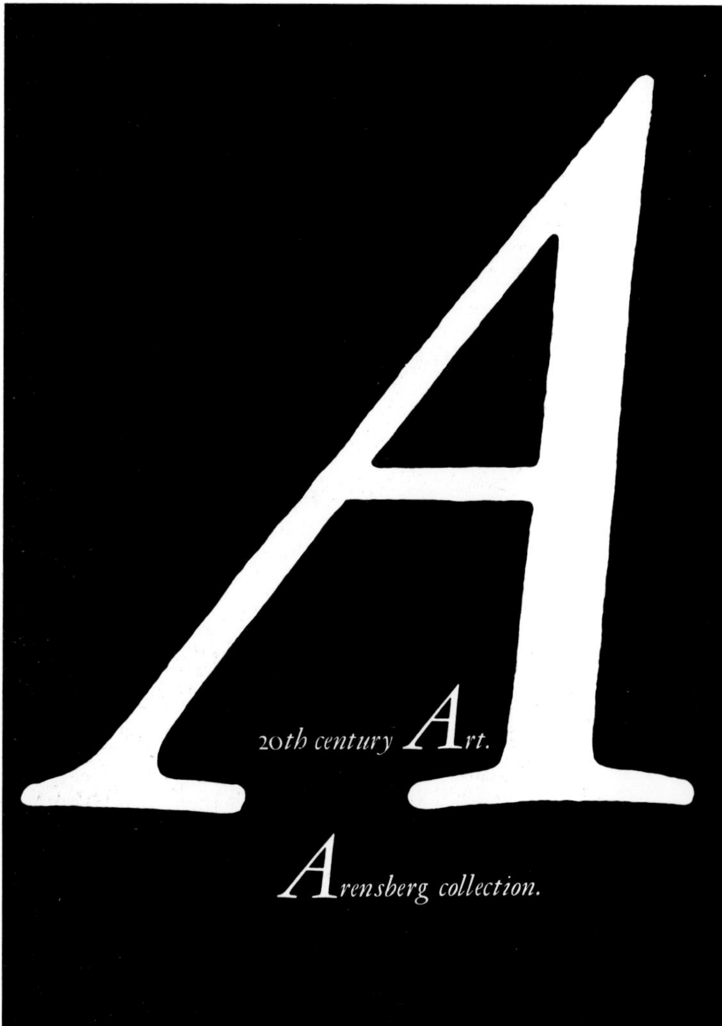
A
20th century Art.
Arensberg collection.

THOMAS ERSKINE on the Advantages of Free Speech
When men can freely communicate their thoughts and their sufferings, real or imaginary, their passions spend themselves in air, like gunpowder scattered upon the surface; but pent up by terrors, they work unseen, burst forth in a moment, and destroy everything in their course.
(Rex v.Paine,1792)
Paul Rand

Great Ideas of Western Man...(one of a series) CONTAINER CORPORATION OF AMERICA

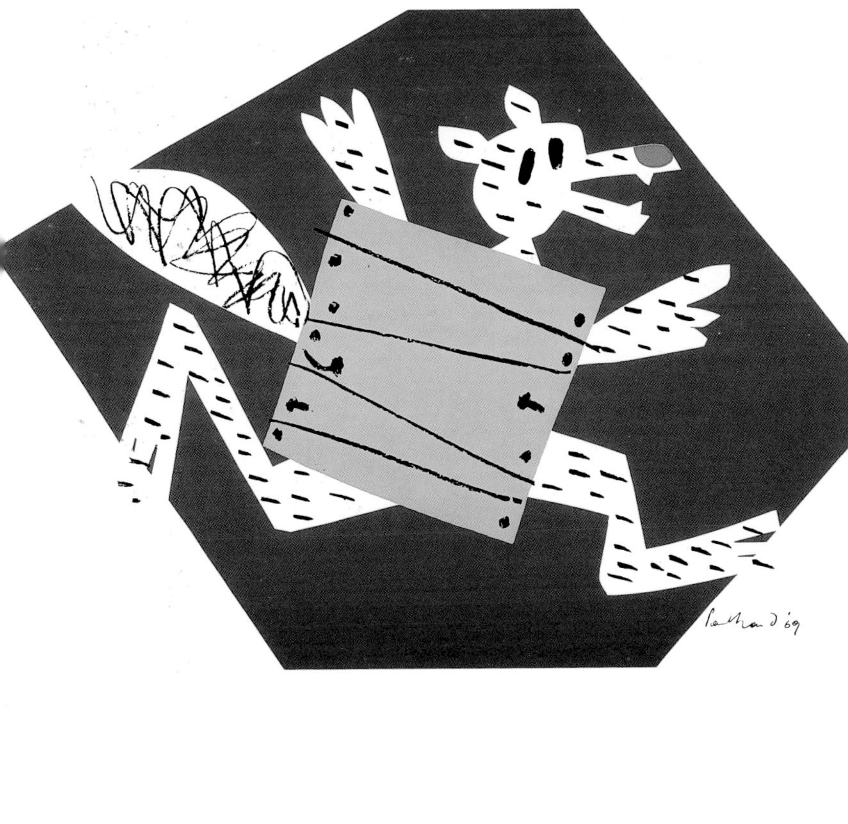

Oh
I know
such
a
lot
of
things,
but
as
I
grow
I know
I'll
know
much
more.

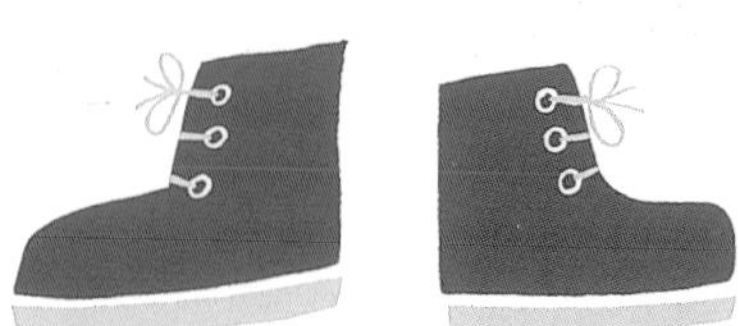

EL PRODUCTO
santa's favorite cigar
EL PRODUCTO
G.H.P.Co
Paul Rand

234

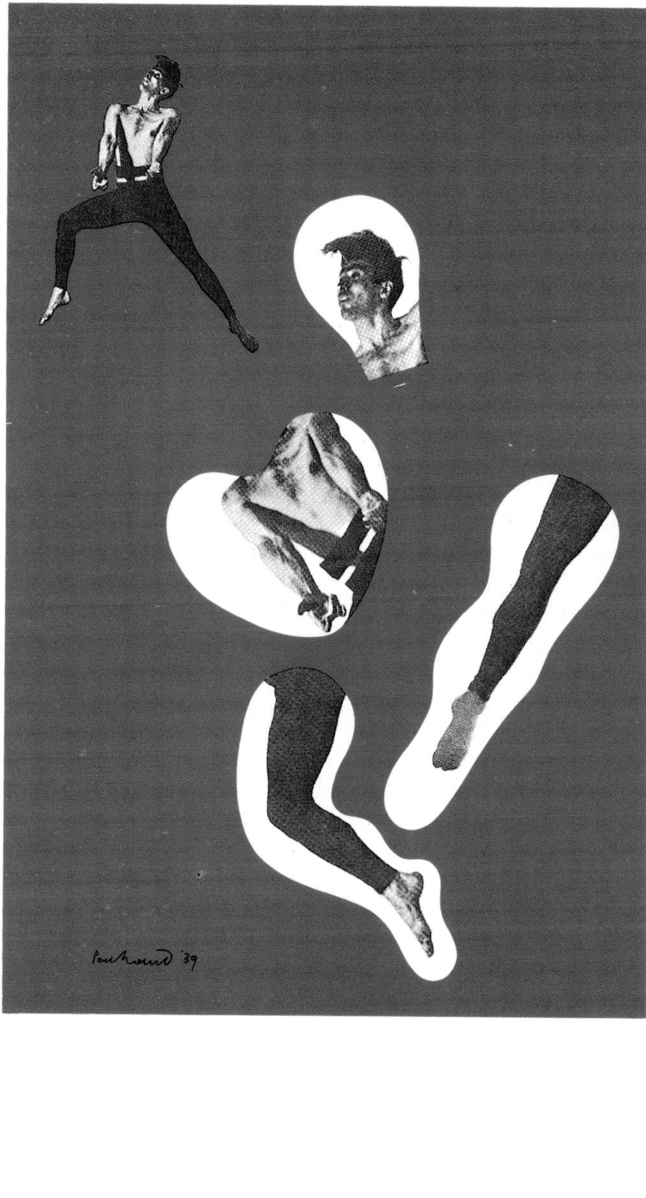

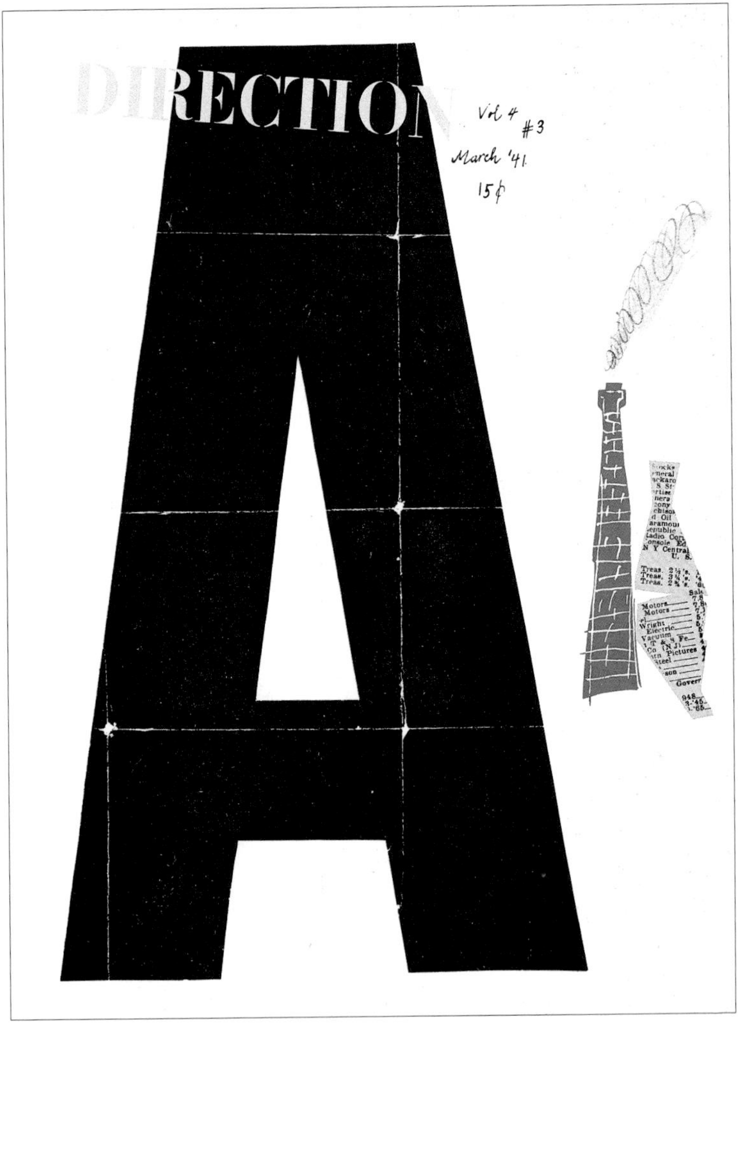
DIRECTION
Vol 4
#3
March '41
15¢

Hollywood Number*
DIRECTION
15¢
April 1940
Vol. 3, No 4
!

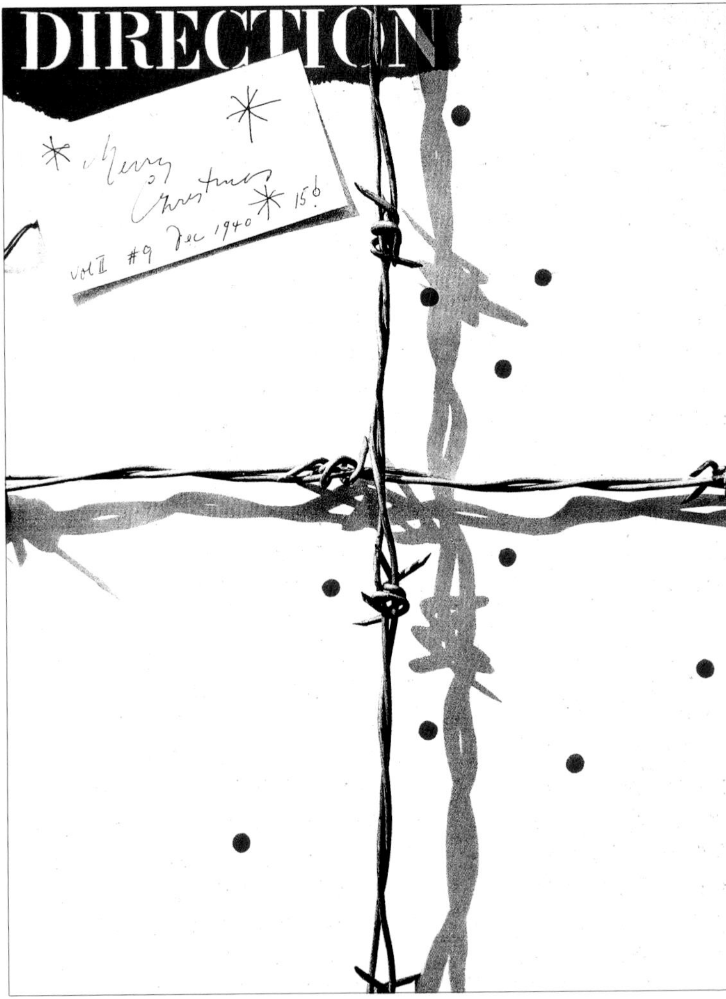
DIRECTION
Merry Christmas
15¢
Vol II #9 Dec 1940

238

Paul Rand was born in 1914. He studied at Pratt Institute, Parsons School of Design, and the Art Students League, under George Gross. At twenty-three, he became the art director of *Esquire* and subsequently spent thirteen years as creative director of a New York advertising agency. He was a consultant to IBM, Cummins Engine Company, and, for many years, Westinghouse Electric Corporation.

He was the author of *Thoughts on Design*, *Design and the Play Instinct*, *The Trademarks of Paul Rand*, and *A Paul Rand Miscellany*, as well as numerous papers on design, art, and typography. His most recent book, *Paul Rand: A Designer's Art*, was published by Yale University Press in the fall of 1985. Beginning in 1956 Rand taught at Yale University School of Art; he served there as professor emeritus of graphic design. For two decades of his career he taught in the Yale summer school program in Brissago, Switzerland, until his death in 1996.

Rand's work is in the permanent collections of many museums in the United States, Europe, and Japan. He received awards for the design of advertisements, brochures, and children's book illustrations.

AWARDS AND HONORS

Honorary Degrees: Doctor of Fine Arts from the Philadelphia College of Art; Parsons School of Design; University of Hartford; School of Visual Arts. Doctor of Letters: Kutztown University. Master of Arts: Yale University; Gold Medals and Hall of Fame member at the New York Art Directors Club; Royal Designer for Industry, Royal Society, London; Gold Medal AIGA; Medal, Type Directors Club; Medal, University of Hartford; President's Fellow, Rhode Island School of Design; Honorary Professor, Tama University, Tokyo, Japan; First Florence Prize for Visual Communication.

5

IKKO tanaka

WITH A METAPHOR

by TAKAHASHI MUTSUO, poet

TO SPEAK DIRECTLY OF AN EXISTENCE LIKE THAT OF IKKO TANAKA IS DIFFICULT. NO, IT IS ALMOST IMPOSSIBLE. LET US USE THE INDIRECT METHOD, THE METAPHOR.

When I think of Tanaka, there is an image I always associate him with: that of a mountain. A large mountain, but not the steep kind that intimidates people. Infinitely gentle, sloping, this mountain accepts climbers, with a great many starting points for the ascent. We may refer to those various starting points as the logotype, the poster, the calendar, book design, graphic art, or total image making. The climber may take any starting point for his ascent. Any starting point will lead him up, and he will never tire of the rich scenery along the way.

However, it would be a mistake to assume that by climbing the mountain one has understood it. The further up one goes, the deeper in one goes, the mountain's height

only increases; its recesses only deepen, and the mountain soars beyond measurement.

Referring to Nara, Japan, where Tanaka spent his childhood, I am tempted to call that mountain Mount Mikasa. At present, Mount Mikasa rises 966 feet, a mere foothill of Mount Kasuga. But when Abe no Nakamaro, during his sojourn at Chang An, the capital of T'ang China, spoke of it as "Mount Mikasa of Kasuga," it was one with the 1,644-foot high Mount Kasuga, behind it.

And Mount Kasuga was part of the broad Kasagi mountain range behind it. The Kasagi mountain range itself passed through the Ryumon range, and was one with the mountains of Yoshino and Kumano. And Mount Yoshino, as legend had it, encompassed all mountains, not only of Japan, but imagistically of the entire world.

Thus the grandeur of this mountain is not a matter of mere steepness. It is large because of its power to encompass. Many of the designers of the present age attempt to actualize the self by excluding historical and contemporary references, but not Tanaka. Tanaka accepts many others, and by letting each of the others express himself he actualizes the transcendent individuality that is unmistakably Ikko Tanaka. Such, to be sure, is the fundamental character of the art director, and yet just as surely one cannot find another who is an art director in the sense that Tanaka is. Recently Tanaka has begun a movement to draw Japanese artists from all genres into

the recreation of the spirit of the tea ceremony. It is unthinkable that any other figure in the present age could accomplish such a feat. Searching through history, one recalls the name of perhaps one other similar figure, Honami Koetsu.*

One asks who achieves the greatest growth through this movement, and the answer is Tanaka himself. Returning to the metaphor of the mountain, we may say that this great mountain is always gentle, and even now is constantly growing.

*A celebrated calligrapher and painter during Japan's Edo period.

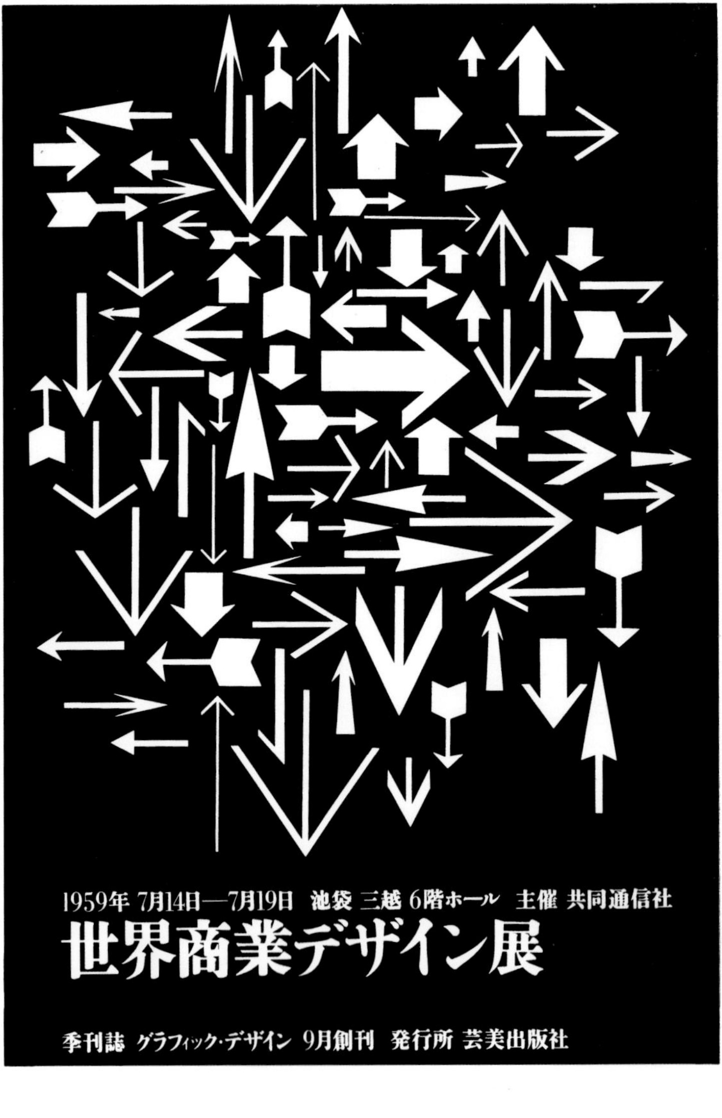
1959年 7月14日—7月19日 池袋 三越 6階ホール 主催 共同通信社
世界商業デザイン展
季刊誌 グラフィック・デザイン 9月創刊 発行所 芸美出版社

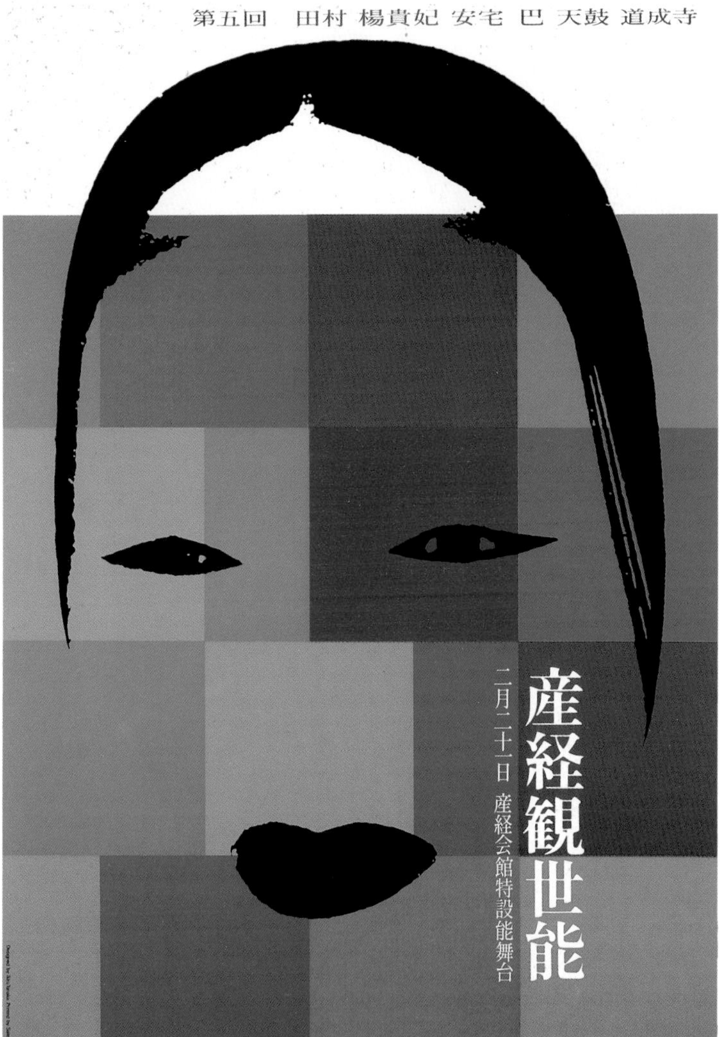
第五回　田村 楊貴妃 安宅 巴 天鼓 道成寺
産経観世能
二月二十一日 産経会館特設能舞台

第八回産経観世能

第一部十時始

観世静夫

一角仙人 観世寿夫

梅若泰之

花筐 梅若六郎

舞囃子 唐船 橋岡久太郎

安宅 観世喜之

第二部四時始

実盛 観世銕之丞

観世元昭

草子洗小町 観世元正

土蜘蛛 梅若猶義

梅若万三郎

昭和三十六年二月二十六日(日)

大阪産経会館特設能舞台

主催 産経新聞社 大阪新聞社

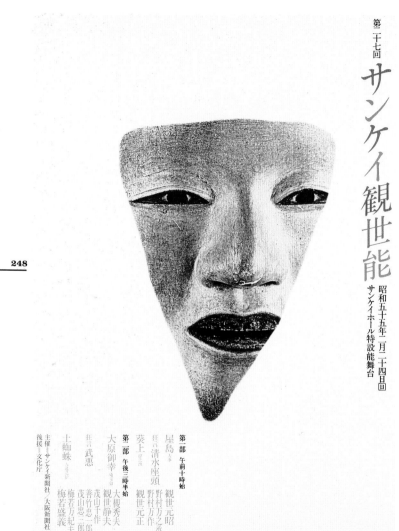

第二十七回

サンケイ観世能

昭和五十五年二月二十四日（日）
サンケイホール特設能舞台

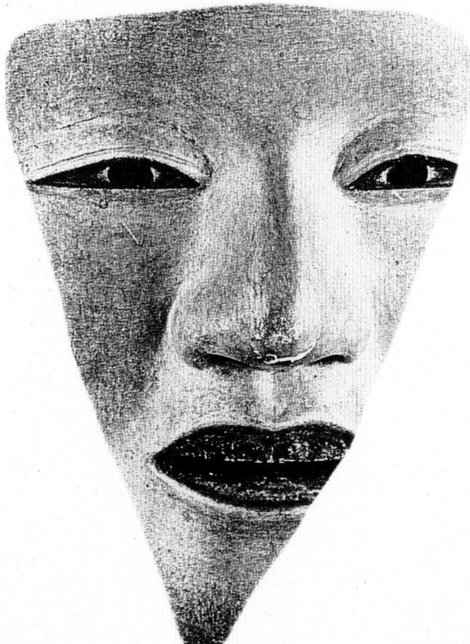

第一部　午前十時始

屋島（大事）　観世元昭

狂言　清水座頭　野村万之丞／野村万作

葵上（梓之出）　観世元正

第二部　午後三時半始

大原御幸（庵室留）　大槻秀夫／観世静夫

狂言　武悪　茂山千作／善竹忠一郎／茂山忠三郎

土蜘蛛（入違之伝）　梅若万紀夫／梅若盛義

主催＝サンケイ新聞社／大阪新聞社
後援＝文化庁

第二十八回
サンケイ観世能
昭和五十六年十二月二十二日(日) サンケイホール特設能舞台
第一部
通小町
雨夜之伝
梅若六之丞
梅若恭行
狂言
子盗人
善竹忠一郎
揚貴妃
台留
観世元昭
第二部
班女
笹之伝
観世元正
狂言
木六駄
茂山千作
望月
古式
観世銕之丞

250

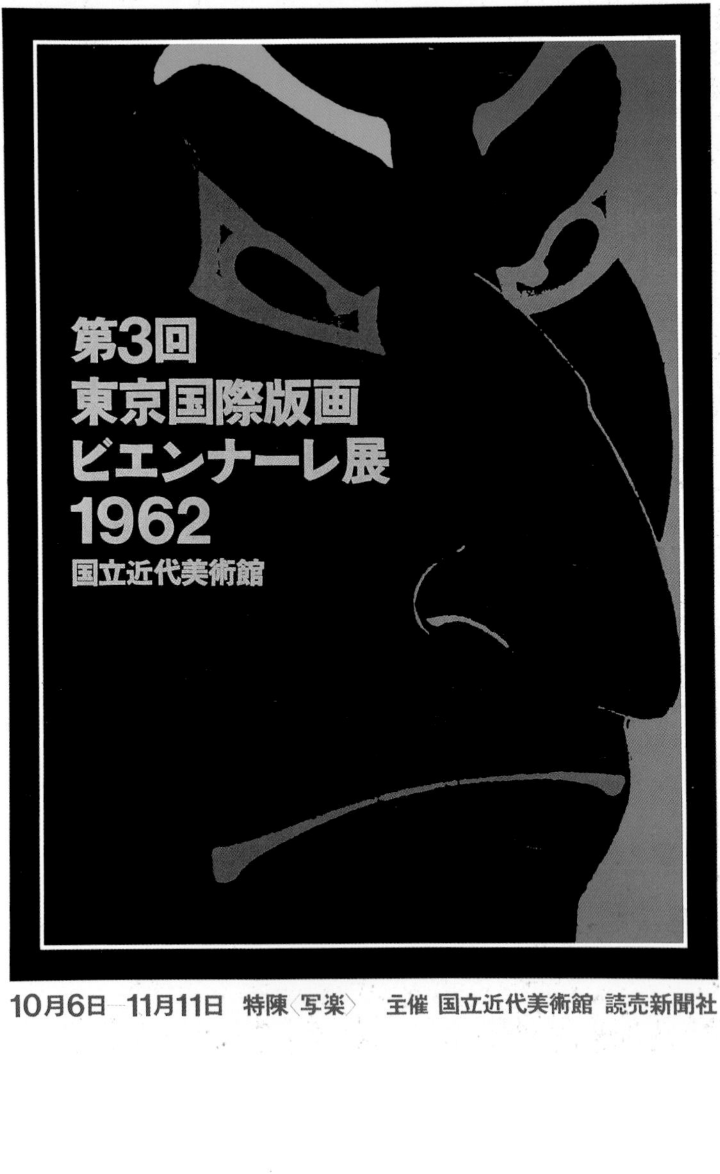
第3回
東京国際版画
ビエンナーレ展
1962
国立近代美術館
10月6日—11月11日 特陳〈写楽〉 主催 国立近代美術館 読売新聞社

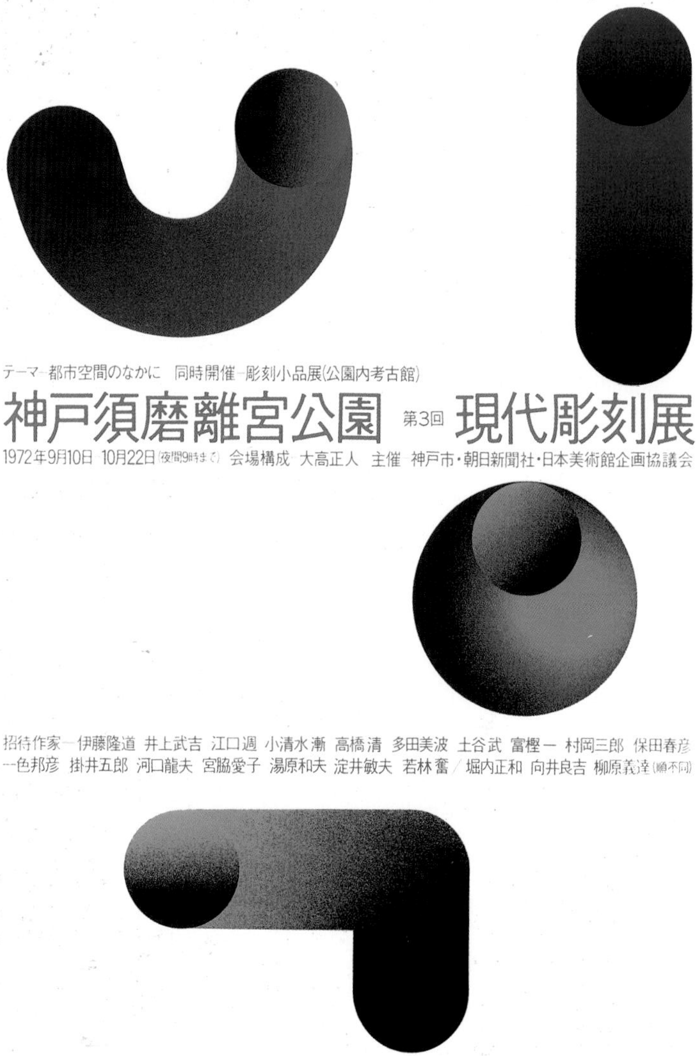
テーマ―都市空間のなかに　同時開催―彫刻小品展(公園内考古館)
神戸須磨離宮公園
第3回
現代彫刻展
1972年9月10日―10月22日(夜間9時まで)　会場構成―大高正人　主催―神戸市・朝日新聞社・日本美術館企画協議会
招待作家―伊藤隆道　井上武吉　江口週　小清水漸　高橋清　多田美波　土谷武　富樫一　村岡三郎　保田春彦
一色邦彦　掛井五郎　河口龍夫　宮脇愛子　湯原和夫　淀井敏夫　若林奮／堀内正和　向井良吉　柳原義達(順不同)

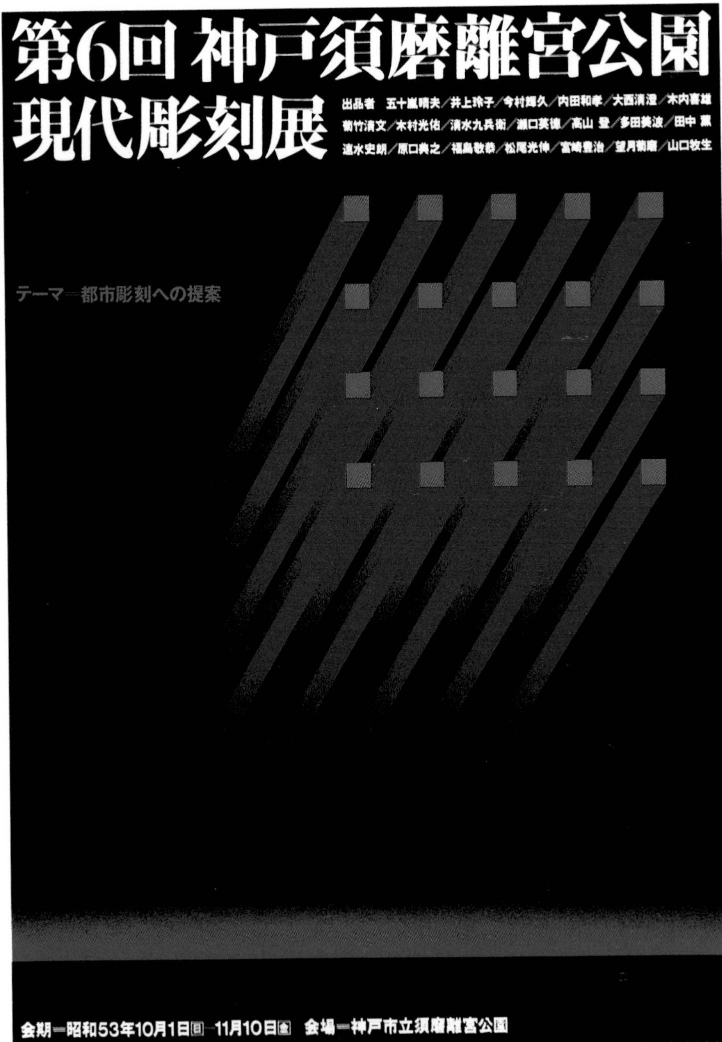
第6回 神戸須磨離宮公園
現代彫刻展
出品者 五十嵐晴夫／井上玲子／今村輝久／内田和孝／大西清澄／木内喜雄
菊竹清文／木村光佑／清水九兵衛／瀬口英徳／高山 登／多田美波／田中 薫
速水史朗／原口典之／福島敬恭／松尾光伸／宮崎豊治／望月菊磨／山口牧生
テーマ＝都市彫刻への提案
会期＝昭和53年10月1日(日)－11月10日(金) 会場＝神戸市立須磨離宮公園
主催＝神戸市／日本美術館企画協議会／朝日新聞社 入選候補作品(エスキース)展 昭和53年10月5日(木)－10月10日(火) ギャラリーさんちか

253

POSTER
NIPPON
POSTER NIPPON 1955-'72
Japanese Posters by Screen Process
Circulated by
International Exhibitions Foundation
United States of America

池坊専永展
こころを生ける
銀座松坂屋開店五〇年記念
三月二十日(木)—三月二十六日(火)
銀座松坂屋　七階大会場
入場料—二〇〇円　主催—華道家元　池坊総務所

IDENTITY

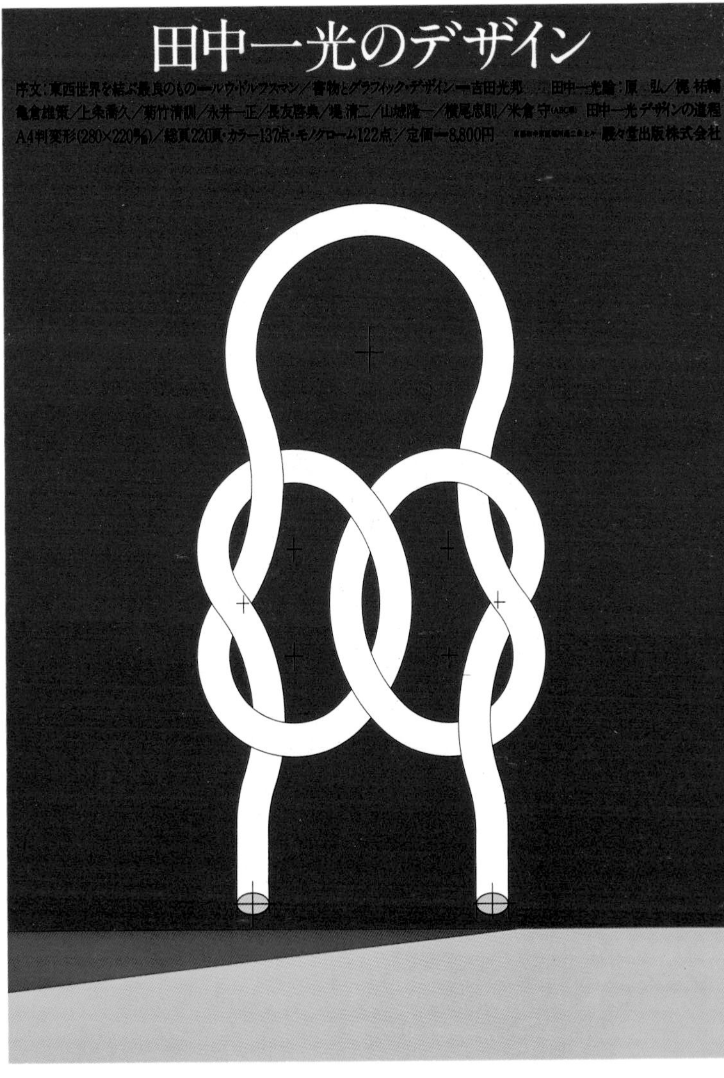
田中一光のデザイン
序文：東西世界を結ぶ最良のもの—ルウ・ドルフスマン／書物とグラフィック・デザイン—吉田光邦　田中一光論：原 弘／梶 祐輔
亀倉雄策／上条喬久／菊竹清訓／永井一正／長友啓典／堤 清二／山城隆一／横尾忠則／米倉 守(ABC順)　田中一光デザインの道程
A4判変形(280×220ミリ)／総頁220頁・カラー137点・モノクローム122点／定価—8,800円　駸々堂出版株式会社

257

dance today '75

'60年代以後、新たな肉体の発見に挑む！ ニューヨーク・アヴァンギャルド——ポスト・モダンダンス。

12月12日(金) P.M.6:30
Trisha Brown/Simone Forti
トリシャ・ブラウン
シモーヌ・フォルティ

12月13日(土) P.M.6:30
Bonjin Atsugi/David Gordon
厚木凡人
デイヴィッド・ゴードン

12月14日(日) P.M.1:30
Suzushi Hanayagi/Grand Union
花柳寿々紫
グランド・ユニオン

12月15日(月) P.M.6:30
Suzushi Hanayagi/Trisha Brown
花柳寿々紫
トリシャ・ブラウン

12月16日(火) P.M.6:30
David Gordon/Simone Forti
デイヴィッド・ゴードン
シモーヌ・フォルティ

12月17日(水) P.M.6:30
Bonjin Atsugi/Grand Union
厚木凡人
グランド・ユニオン

主催 パルコ/後援 アメリカン センター

入場料 3000円(全席自由)
前売所 西武劇場プレイガイド(渋谷パルコ1F)/都内各プレイガイド
電話予約 464-5111内60 お問い合せ 西武劇場464-5100-1

西武劇場

照明 小松哲夫/舞台監督 田原進

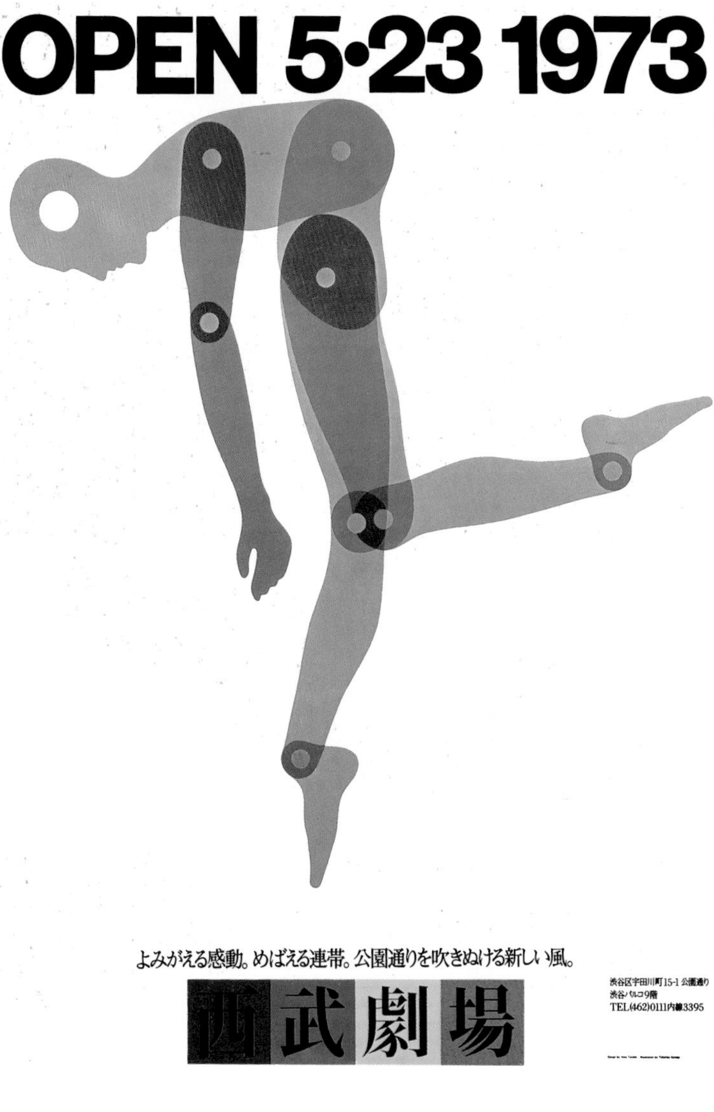
OPEN 5•23 1973
よみがえる感動。めばえる連帯。公園通りを吹きぬける新しい風。
西武劇場
渋谷区宇田川町15-1 公園通り
渋谷パルコ9階
TEL(462)0111内線3395

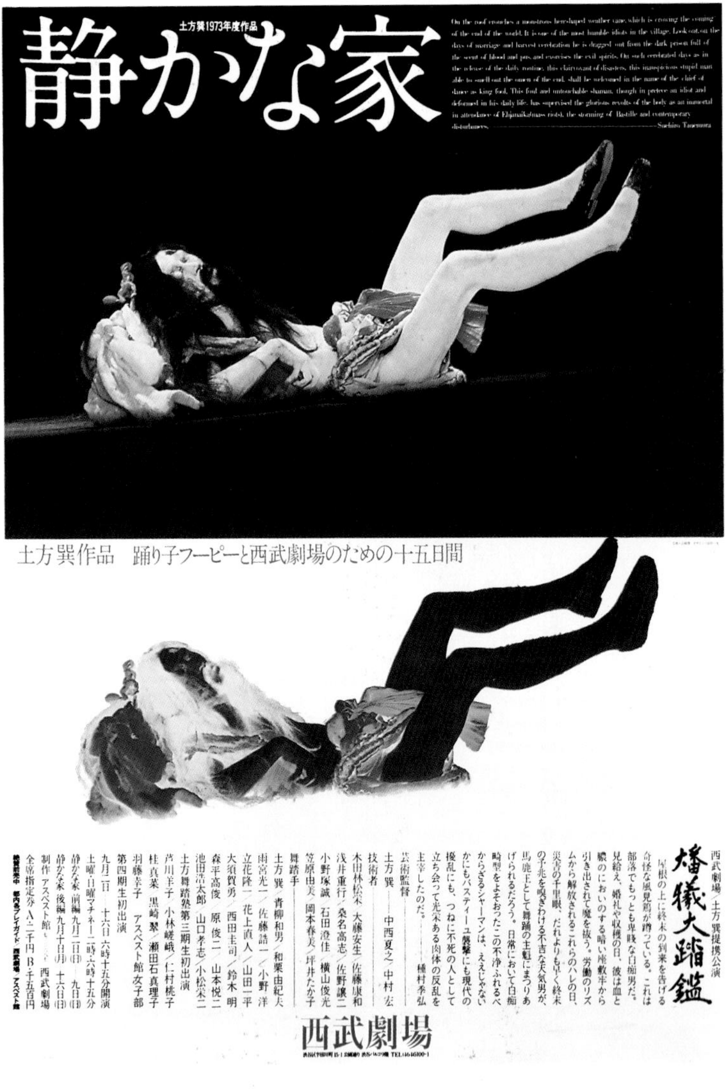
土方巽1973年度作品
静かな家
On the roof crouches a monstrous hen-shaped weather vane, which is crowing the coming of the end of the world. It is one of the most humble idiots in the village. Look out, on the days of marriage and harvest celebration he is dragged out from the dark prison full of the scent of blood and pus, and exorcises the evil spirits. On such celebrated days as in the release of the daily routine, this clairvoyant of disasters, this inauspicious stupid man able to smell out the omen of the end, shall be welcomed in the name of the chief of dance as king fool. This fool and untouchable shaman, though in pretece an idiot and deformed in his daily life, has supervised the glorious revolts of the body as an immortal in attendance of Ehjanaika(mass riots), the storming of Bastille and contemporary disturbances. ——Suehiro Tanemura
土方巽作品　踊り子フーピーと西武劇場のための十五日間
西武劇場／土方巽提携公演
燔犧大踏鑑
屋根の上に終末の到来を告げる奇怪な風見鶏が蹲っている。これは部落でもっとも卑賤な白痴男だ。見給え、婚礼や収穫の日、彼は血と膿のにおいのする暗い座敷牢から引き出されて魔を祓う。労働のリズムから解放されるこれらのハレの日、災害の千里眼、だれよりも早く終末の予兆を嗅ぎわける不吉な天気男が、馬鹿王として舞踊の主魁にまつりあげられるだろう。日常において白痴畸型をよそおったこの不浄ふれるべからざるシャーマンは、ええじゃないかにもバスティーユ襲撃にも現代の擾乱にも、つねに不死の人として立ち会って光栄ある肉体の反乱を主宰したのだ。——種村季弘
芸術監督
土方巽——中西夏之／中村宏
技術者
木田林松栄／大藤安生／佐藤康和
浅井重行／桑名高志／佐野譲二
小野塚誠／石田澄佳／横山俊光
笠原由美／岡本春美／坪井たか子
舞踏手
土方巽／青柳和男／和栗由紀夫
雨宮光一／佐藤詰一／小野洋
立花隆一／花上直人／山田一平
大須賀勇／西田圭司／鈴木明
森平高俊／原俊二／山本悦二
池田浩太郎／山口孝志／小松栄二
土方舞踏塾第三期生初出演
芦川羊子／小林嵯峨／仁村桃子
桂真菜／黒崎翠／瀬田石真理子
羽藤幸子　アスベスト館女子部
第四期生初出演
九月二日——十六日　六時十五分開演
土曜・日曜マチネー二時・六時十五分
静かな家　前編　九月二日(日)——九日(日)
静かな家　後編　九月十日(月)——十六日(日)
制作　アスベスト館　西武劇場
全席指定券　A・二千円　B・千五百円
絶賛前売中　都内各プレイガイド／西武劇場／アスベスト館
西武劇場
TEL(464)5100-1

西武劇場プロデュース公演 十二月二十一日—二十三日
上方芸の会
ご案内—小沢昭一／永 六輔
狂言 二十一日(金)午後六時三十分開演
独り松茸— 茂山千之丞
花子— 茂山千之丞／茂山千五郎／茂山正義
蝸牛— 茂山千作／茂山千五郎／茂山千之丞
茂山千之丞
舞 二十二日
吉村雄輝
落語 二十三日
桂 米朝
お問い合せ 西武劇場
絶賛前売中 入場料 全席
円
都内各プレイガイド
西武劇場
Design by Ikko Tanaka

MUSIC TODAY '85
「今日の音楽」·13
企画・構成＝武満 徹
制作：西武セゾングループ
制作協力：東京コンサーツ
1985年6月25日(火)～30日(日)・西武劇場
入場料 前売券 2,700円 当日券 3,000円 全自由席
お問い合わせ 東京コンサーツ TEL 03-359-9755
6月25日火 19:00
ロンドン・シンフォニエッタ演奏会(1)
ウィトルト・ルトスワウスキ チェイン1
ナイジェル・オズボーン ザンサ
武満 徹 レイン・カミング
ハリソン・バートウィスル シークレット・シアター
演奏 ロンドン・シンフォニエッタ
指揮 エルガー・ハワース
6月26日水 19:00
ロンドン・シンフォニエッタ演奏会(2)
ジョージ・ベンジャミン アット・ファースト・ライト
ハンス・エイブラムセン メルヘンビルダー
ロビン・ホロウェイ ショウピース
ヤニス・クセナキス サレイン
演奏 ロンドン・シンフォニエッタ
指揮 エルガー・ハワース
6月27日木 19:00
松平頼暁作品演奏会
アセンブリッジ 糸のための(1968)(ステージ初演)
シミュレーション チューバのための(1974 75)
サルヴェ・レジナ(1981)
ツェルカ 2本のフルートのための(1980)
ブレンディング ピアノのための(1984)
レクイエム・セクラレム(1985・初演)
6月28日金 19:00
木村かをりピアノリサイタル
クラウド・アトラス(1985・初演)
ドビュッシー 「エチュード」より
メシアン 「鳥のカタログ」より
ベルク 室内協奏曲(ベルク生誕100年・没後50年記念)
ピアノ独奏 木村かをり
6月29日土 19:00
F・ジェフスキー作品演奏会
マシーン(ピアノデュオ)
ウィンズボロ・コットンミル・ブルース(ピアノデュオ)
アリア(フルートソロ)
メアリーズ・ドリーム
マヤコフスキー
ソング・アンド・ダンス
6月30日日 14:30
第2回「今日の音楽・作曲賞」コンクール本選コンサート
ホープ・リー メルボアク
コート・リップ デュオ・ピアノ・ミュージック
フランコ・ハリアナ ダ・コシ・トッタ・マン…
レイムンド・ユーソッヒ オブセッション
フルート・ソロのための「線」
マルチン・フォセヴィツ フルート・ソロのための「サナトス」
コンチェルト
アントニオ・ジャコメッティ レリカ
アントニオ・ローチェ フラーメン
9人の奏者のための「ヴェリスモ」
お問い合わせ 東京コンサーツ 03-359-9755
PARCO 西武劇場

歌舞伎の発見 誰でもわかる歌舞伎の見方
富田鉄之助著 白金書房刊
助六由縁江戸桜勧進帳鳴神矢の根毛抜解脱不破嬔
暫不動象引寿曽我対面菅原伝授手習鑑 神霊矢口渡
国性爺合戦 蘆屋道満大内鑑 嫗山姥 小野道風青柳硯
仮名手本忠臣蔵 平家女護島 傾城反魂香 義経千本桜
博多小女郎浪枕 源平布引滝 一谷嫩軍記 壇浦兜軍記
奥州安達原 鬼一法眼三略巻 八陣守護城 忍夜恋曲者
御所桜堀川夜討 祇園祭礼信仰記 加賀見山旧錦絵
本朝廿四孝 鎌倉三代記 妹背山婦女庭訓 絵本太功記
敵討天下茶屋聚 伊賀越道中双六 近江源氏先陣館
恋女房染分手綱 摂州合邦辻 伽羅先代萩 楼門五三桐
曾根崎心中 近頃河原の達引 桂川連理柵 艶容女舞衣
天竺徳兵衛韓噺 東海道四谷怪談 双蝶々曲輪日記
女殺油地獄 大経師昔暦 恋飛脚大和往来 新版歌祭文
生写朝顔話 心中天網島 伊達娘恋緋鹿子 積恋雪関扉
夏祭浪花鑑 伊勢音頭恋寝刃 廓文章 お染の七役 茨木
京鹿子娘道成寺 連獅子 草摺引 素襖落 土蜘蛛 紅葉狩
春興鏡獅子 六歌仙容彩 船弁慶 舌出三番叟 釣女 藤娘
与話情浮名横櫛 色彩間苅豆 乗合船恵方万歳 三社祭
四千両小判梅葉 水天宮利生深川 十六夜清心 吉原雀
籠釣瓶花街酔醒 神明裏和合取組 五大力恋緘 手習子
人情咄文七元結 怪異談牡丹燈籠 佐倉義民伝 鳥羽絵
蔦紅葉宇都谷峠 東海道中膝栗毛 明烏花濡衣 神田祭
天衣紛上野初花 梅雨小袖昔八丈 天一坊大岡政談 黒塚
盲長屋梅加賀鳶 巷談宵宮雨 元禄忠臣蔵 名月八幡祭
刺青奇偶 桐一葉 番町皿屋敷 一本刀土俵入 双面水照月
沓手鳥孤城落月 鳥辺山心中 修禅寺物語 暗闇の丑松
歌舞伎

265

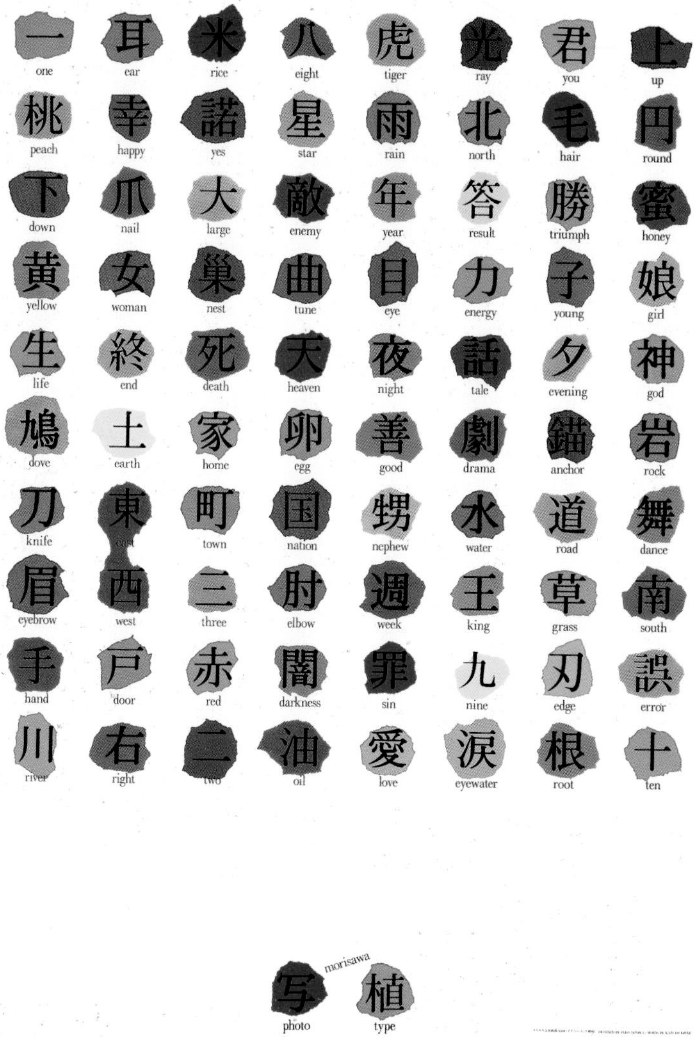
一 one
耳 ear
米 rice
八 eight
虎 tiger
光 ray
君 you
上 up
桃 peach
幸 happy
諾 yes
星 star
雨 rain
北 north
毛 hair
円 round
下 down
爪 nail
大 large
敵 enemy
年 year
答 result
勝 triumph
蜜 honey
黄 yellow
女 woman
巣 nest
曲 tune
目 eye
力 energy
子 young
娘 girl
生 life
終 end
死 death
天 heaven
夜 night
話 tale
夕 evening
神 god
鳩 dove
土 earth
家 home
卵 egg
善 good
劇 drama
錨 anchor
岩 rock
刀 knife
東 east
町 town
国 nation
甥 nephew
水 water
道 road
舞 dance
眉 eyebrow
西 west
三 three
肘 elbow
週 week
王 king
草 grass
南 south
手 hand
戸 door
赤 red
闇 darkness
罪 sin
九 nine
刃 edge
誤 error
川 river
右 right
二 two
油 oil
愛 love
涙 eyewater
根 root
十 ten
写 photo
morisawa
植 type

第10回いけばな日本百傑展　百の「花」は誇りたかく、百の「華」を競う。

出品作家（五十音順）

安達式挿花　安達潮花
日新流　新井日新
有川式いけ花　有川悦子
翠松会　飯村素翠
古流松藤会　池田昌弘
池坊　池坊専永
大和花道　市川光松
大和花道　今泉映草
系真流　猪熊系憙
古流松藤会　上野理彰
小原流　植村春水
古流理恩会　宇田川理登
都古流本流　内田一油
国風華道会　海野彰人
古流松藤会　榎本理福

そうえい流　江見岬樹
正風流　役正風軒
和風古流　大橋泉秀園
古流大観流　大野理瀞
小原流　大貫文夫
広山流　岡田広山
草月流　尾中千草
小原流　小原夏樹
一葉式　粕谷明弘
一葉式　粕谷明光
本古流　香取柳知
艸心流　蒲田素石
芳月流　神尾芳翠
池坊　川上香華
草心流　川崎草心

柴山古流　川浪冷祥
大和花道　川原田湖秀
駿東流　神崎華今
堂心流　木下瀟雲
小原流　工藤和彦
草月流　久保映泉
古流かたばみ会　熊井理総
龍生派　熊沢仙華
古流松月会　小島喜艸
美風池坊　小島美陽
龍生派　後藤喜舟
小原流　五島泰雲
都古流　小林一阿彌
清風瓶華　小室尚翠
古流松藤会　米野理愛

秀抱流　佐藤秀抱
草月流　渋井玲虹
龍生派　島村芳雲
池坊　七五三月窓
春草流　白沢春草
桂古流　新藤華盛
清風瓶華　末野尚霞
池坊　須賀柏葉
古流松藤会　鈴木理藻
御室流　杉崎宜宗
東和華道　関江松風
古流松応会　千羽理芳
小原流　平光波
古流御家派　宝井理湖
艸心流　竹内杏哉
清香流　立原清香

清香流　立原広明
千家古流　田津原楳陽
日本古流　角田一忠
草月流　勅使河原霞
龍生派　長島桂仙
池坊　中村幾次郎
新派古流　花井一柳
清風瓶華　早川研一
草月流　林映里
松風花道会　原田淑水
大和花道　原田春光
古流松葉会　原野理筆
小原流　原悠光
草月流　日向洸一
池坊　藤原幽竹
青蘭流　堀川晶仙

日本古流　細田一弘
雪舟流　増野雪舟
真月池坊　松谷真月
古流崇顕流　宮上崇顕
柳古流　宮下一風
松月堂古流　宮田方圓居
宏道流　望月義耀
遠州流　森一森
秀抱流　森笙抱
草月流　守谷紅沙
清風瓶華　山崎尚采
大和池坊　山本一水
光風流　山本斎月
相阿弥流　横地宗象円
池坊　吉岡晋月
爽風流　渡辺汀華

運営委員

古流松藤会　池田理英
小原流　小原豊雲
池坊　金子霞璋
大和花道　下田天映
草月流　勅使河原蒼風
清風瓶華　早川尚洞
龍生派　吉村華泉

いけばな日本百傑

9月30日［金］―10月5日［水］　入場料―700円

主催―東京新聞・西武美術館　後援―文化庁

西武美術館

西武百貨店 池袋店12階　木曜休館

新古典主義

活字明朝の格調が写植書体として完璧に生まれ変わりました。新しい正調明朝「リュウミン」、そのファミリーの誕生です。「リュウミン」は、戦前、印刷界で定評のあった森川龍文堂書体をもとに、あらためて現代の組版に最も適した写植用明朝としてデザインされたものです。活字明朝の持つ鋭い彫刻刀の冴えを左右のハライや点の形に生かしながら、縦横の直線にソフトなアクセントを持たせた、文字通りの正調明朝の傑作と呼ぶにふさわしい書体です。

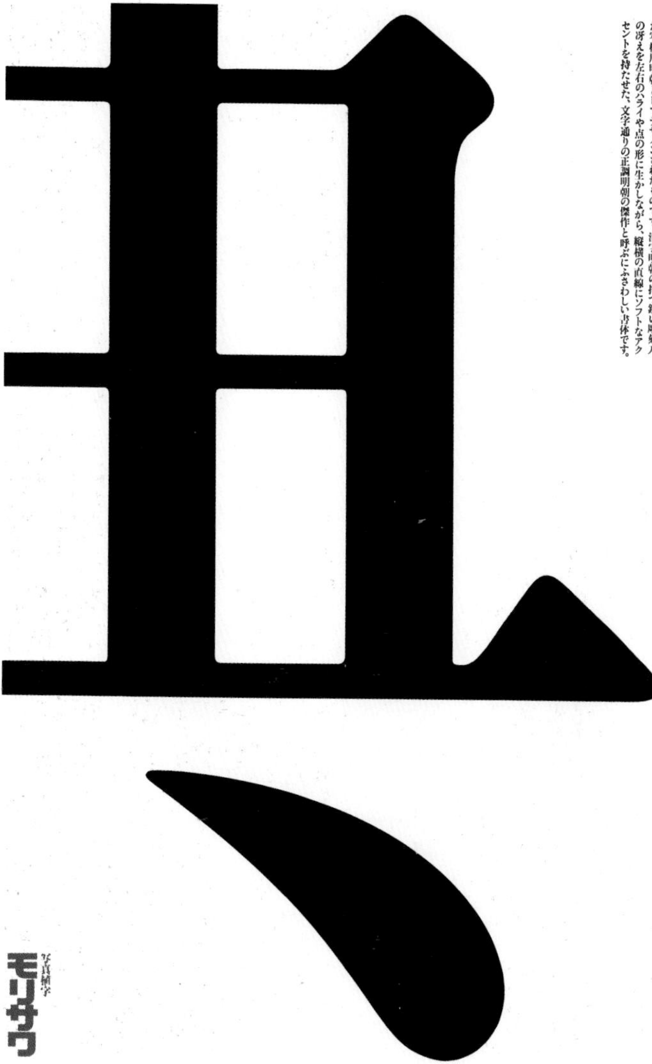

草月
創造
空間
の
展
勅使河原 宏・演出 朝倉 摂・構成
4月24日土—4月30日金
会場=草月会館 A.M.10:00 P.M.5:00
P.M.4:00まで
主催—財団法人草月会 共通鑑賞券—800円
「ホゼイトレース」P.M.1:20 「砂の女」P.M.2:00

270

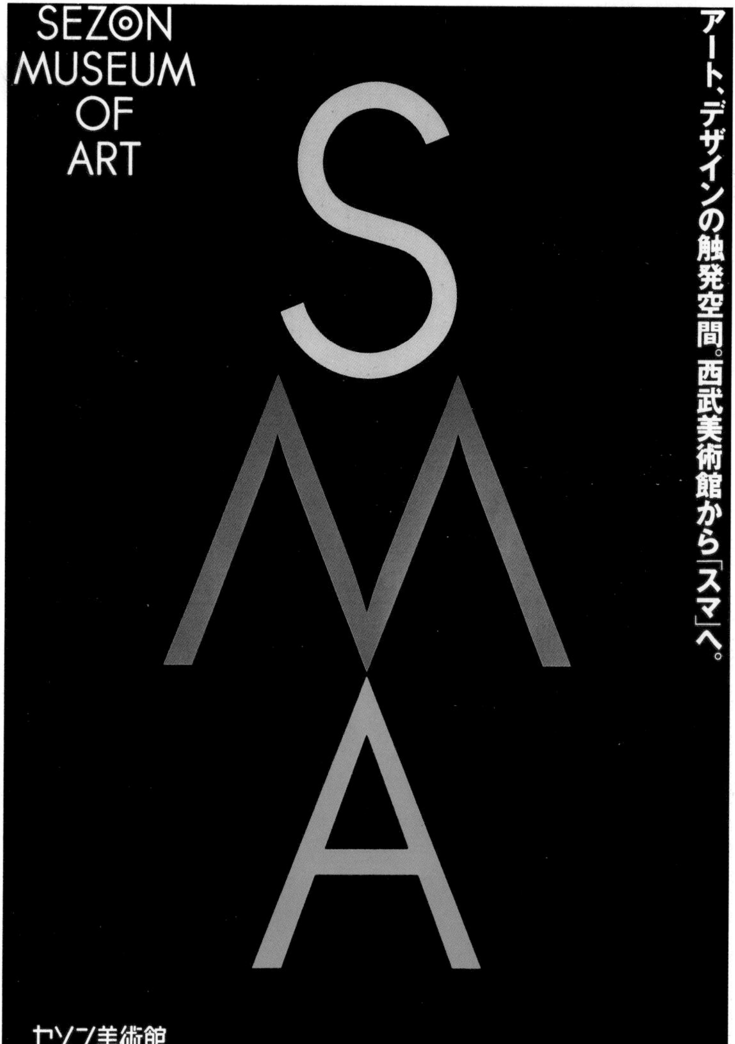
SEZON MUSEUM OF ART
アート、デザインの触発空間。西武美術館から「スマ」へ。
SMA
セゾン美術館
Phone: 03(5992)0155

GINZA SAISON THEATRE
銀座セゾン劇場

新社名の「&」に、気持を入れました。

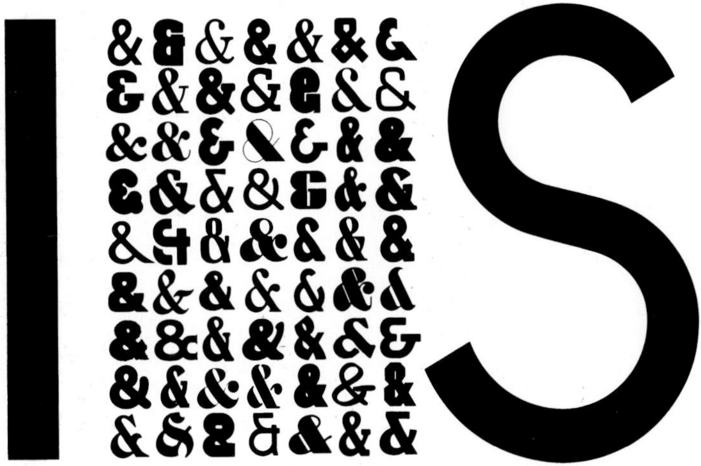

新会社の準備をしつつ、「広告代理店」という言葉が出るたび、どうも私たちはしっくりしないものを感じていました。企業の広告活動の「代理」というニュアンスが、私たちの目ざすところとあまりにも距離がある。こういうことを言うときれいごとに聞こえてしまうのですが、事実、私たちのネットワーク内には、百貨店や劇場やレストランなどもあって、いつも「買う人」「楽しむ人」の前にさらされているわけです。その「苦労」を利用すれば、そういう人々の気持や声を企業の活動に逆流させることはそんなにむずかしくはない。さらに言えば、私たちにはメディア業務や広告制作などの他にも、CIや商品の開発、空間の演出といったちょっと変わった部門まである。これも単に業務の幅を拡げるために設けたわけではなく、それらのすべての部門が集まり、相互に連絡を取りあい、一本の太い血管となることで、企業と生活者の間をよりいっそう緊密にできると思うからです。つまり「&」とは、企業と生活者をトータルな面で「つなぐ」ことを意味している。CFや新聞広告はその一側面にすぎず、私たちの活動のどんなにさ細なことも、すべてが「つなぐ」目的のために生かせることを忘れたくない。新社名にこめたそんな気持を私たち自身も改めてかみしめつつ、スタートを切ります。

株式会社

I&S

JAPAN
CREATIVE
SEIBU
西武
シブヤ
JAPAN
CREATIVE
CREATIVE
JAPAN
CREATIVE

ciao ITALIA
生活が、グラマーです。
9月26日(金)〜10月8日(水)
SAISON
西武セゾングループ
SEIBU
西武

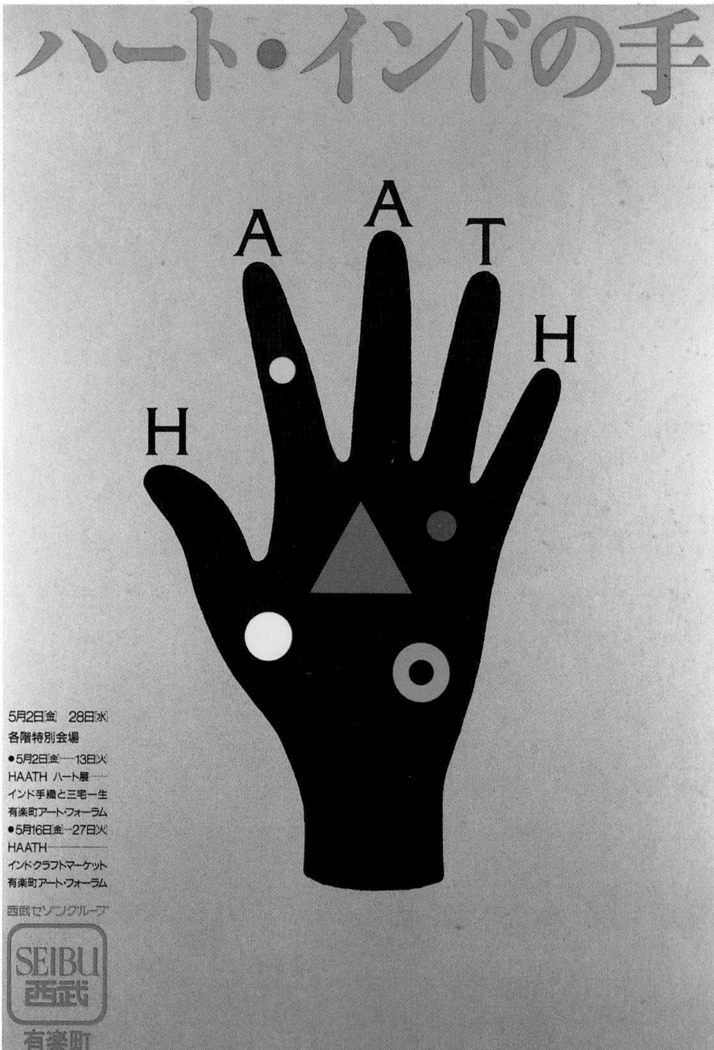
ハート・インドの手
H
A
A
T
H
5月2日[金] 28日[水]
各階特別会場
●5月2日[金]—13日[火]
HAATH ハート展
インド手織と三宅一生
有楽町アート・フォーラム
●5月16日[金]—27日[火]
HAATH
インドクラフトマーケット
有楽町アート・フォーラム
西武セゾングループ
SEIBU
西武
有楽町

書体は分解してみるとその性格が鮮明になる。
モリサワ
MORISAWA & COMPANY LTD.

第16回
全日本
新人
染織展
平成4年1月11日(土)–19日(日)
開室時間…午前10時–午後6時(入場は午後5時半まで)但し常設展の入場は午後8時まで
11日は午後1時半開室・16日休館日 京都市中京区高倉通三条上ル Tel:075-222-0888
京都府 京都文化博物館 5階展示会場
主催…日本きもの染織工芸会 共催…財京都文化財団/日本経済新聞社 後援…通商産業省/文化庁/京都府/京都市/京都商工会議所/NHK京都放送局/(社)日本絹人織織物工業会/(社)全日本きもの振興会 協賛…京都きもの振興会/西陣織工業組合/西陣織物産地問屋協同組合/京都染色協同組合連合会/京都友禅協同組合/(社)日本図案家協会/丹後織物工業組合/加賀染振興協会/京都中央信用金庫 特別協賛…(財)東洋信託文化財団
入場料…一般600円(480円)/大・高生500円(400円)/中・小生400円(320円) ( )内は前売料金

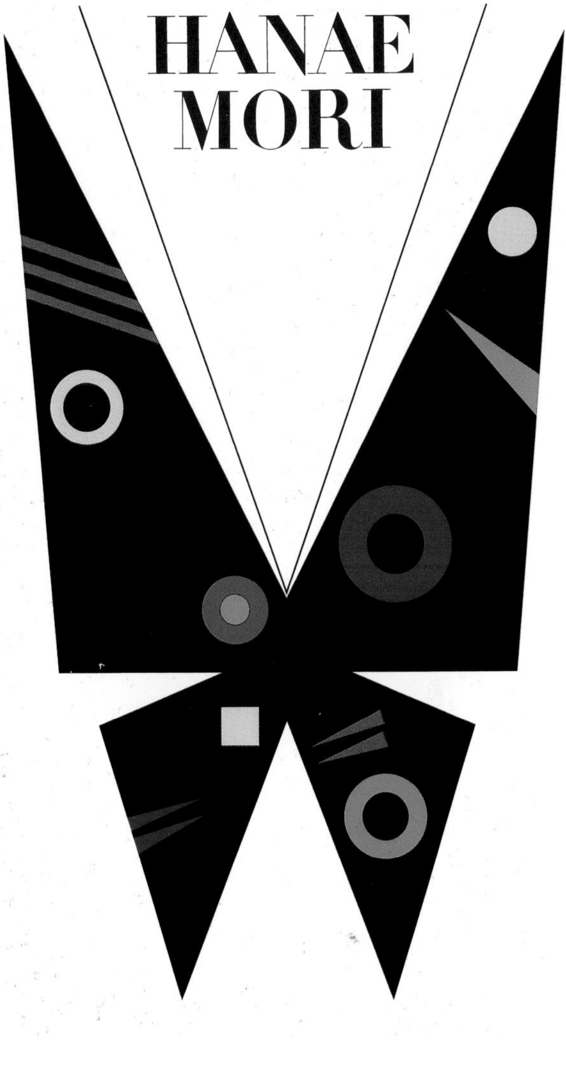

Design by Ikko Tanaka

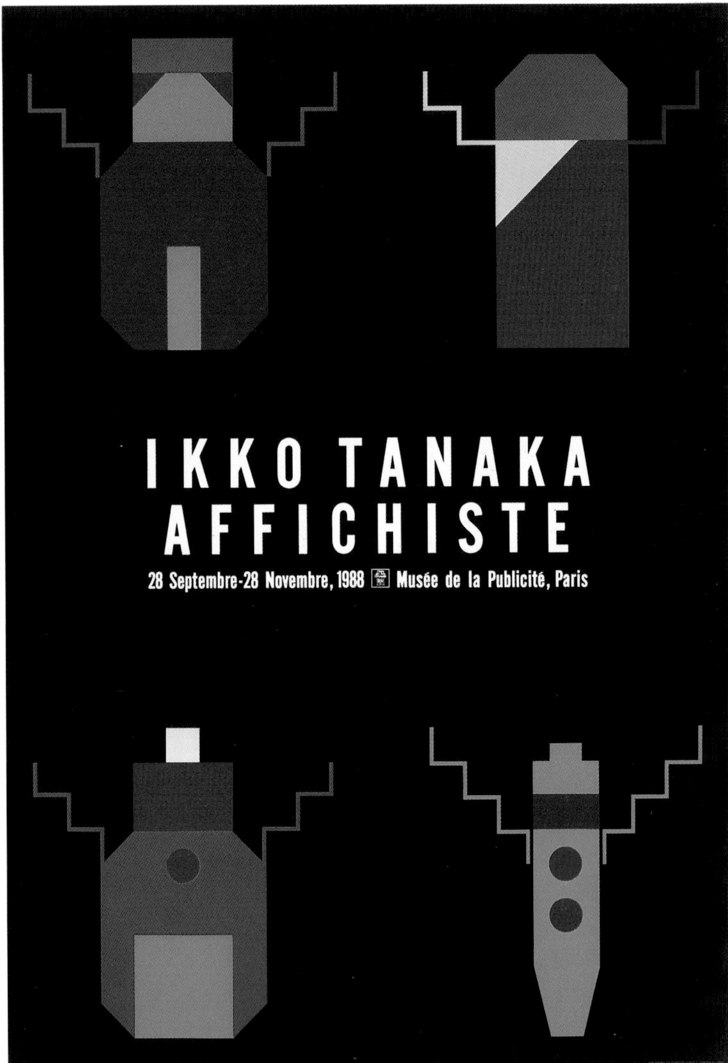
IKKO TANAKA
AFFICHISTE
28 Septembre-28 Novembre, 1988 Musée de la Publicité, Paris

第一回国民文化祭 グランドフィナーレ
ありがとう・日本のこころ
閉会式
第一部…大学生合唱サークルとダークダックスとの競演
第二部…ハイブリッドコンサート
林英哲、竜童組の援助出演を得てジョイント演奏
昭和六十一年十一月二十九日土 午後二時開演
会場…国立劇場(大劇場) 東京都千代田区隼町四一
主催…文化庁/東京都 入場無料
国民文化祭

Nihon Buyo
UCLA
Asian Performing Arts
Institute 1981
Los Angeles
Washington, D.C.
New York

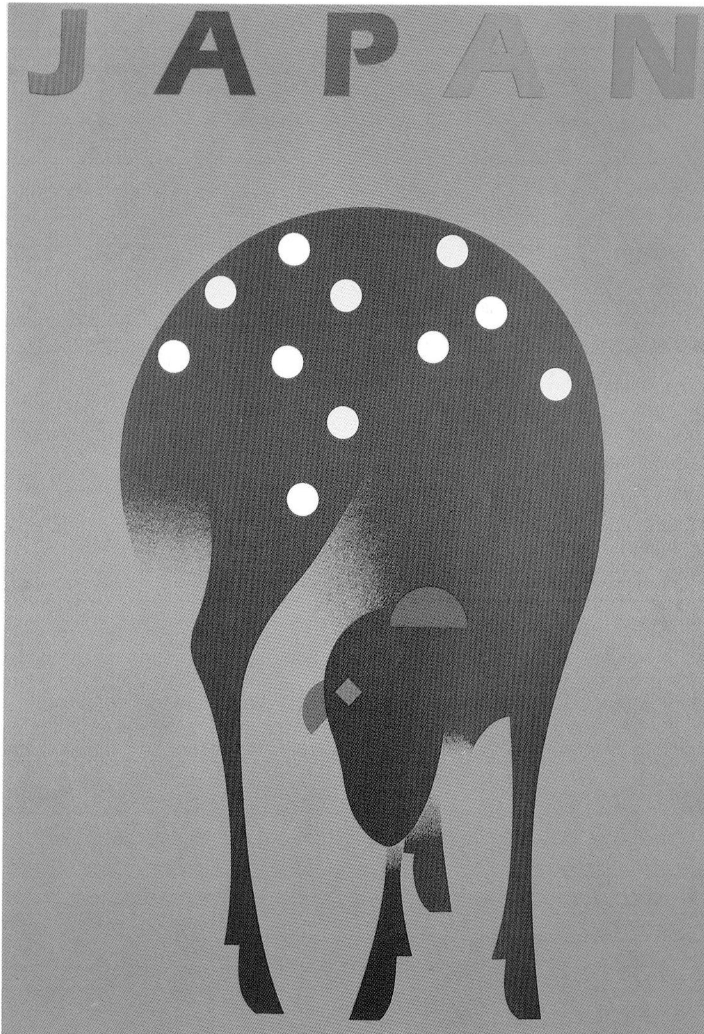
JAPAN

1988
HIROSHIMA
APPEALS
ヒロシマアピールズ
art direction / design / illustration: ikko tanaka
printing: toppan printing co., ltd.
sponsors: hiroshima international cultural foundation, inc.
japan graphic designers association, inc. (jagda)

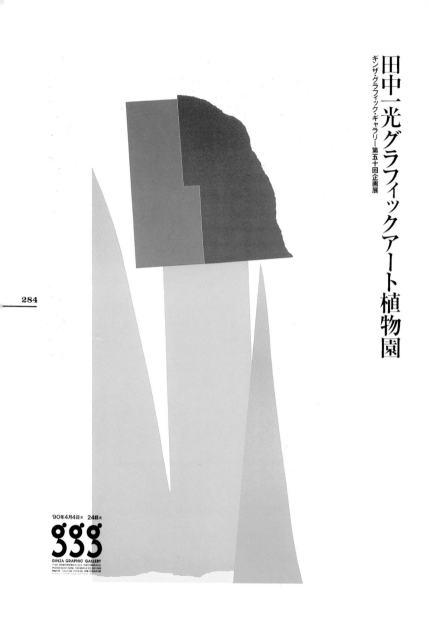

田中一光グラフィックアート植物園
ギンザ・グラフィック・ギャラリー第五十回企画展
'90年4月4日水 24日火
GINZA GRAPHIC GALLERY
PHONE 03 571 5206 FACSIMILE 03 289 1389

285

怖ろしい味
勝見洋一
文藝春秋

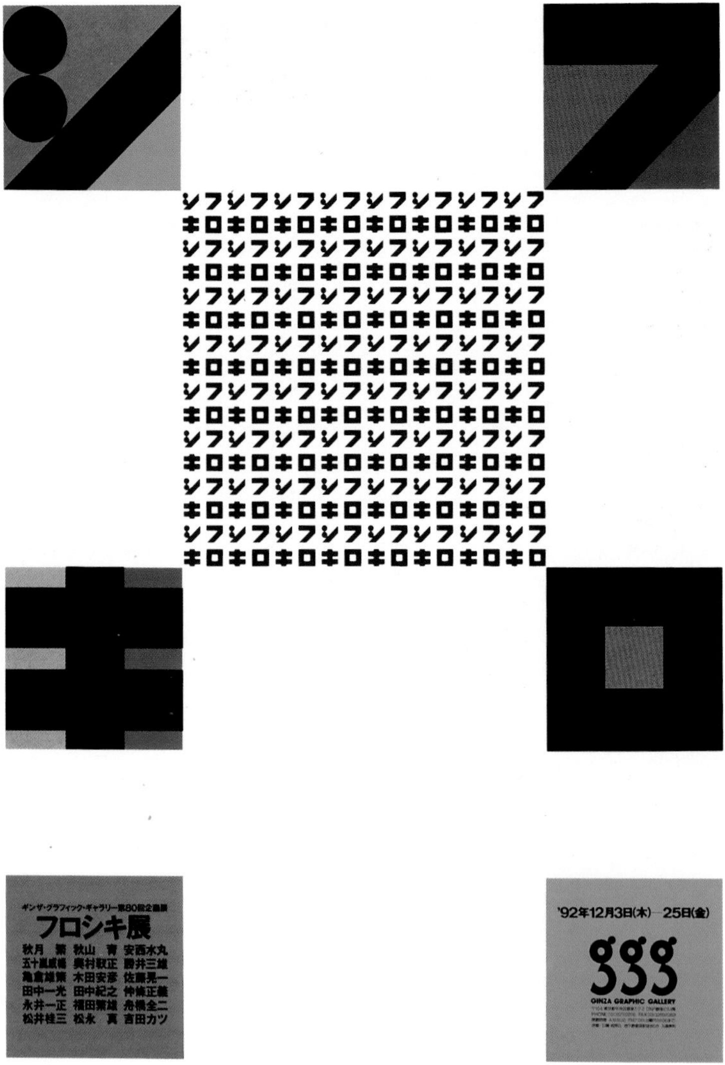
ギンザ・グラフィック・ギャラリー第80回企画展
フロシキ展
秋月 繁 秋山 孝 安西水丸
五十嵐威暢 奥村靫正 勝井三雄
亀倉雄策 木田安彦 佐藤晃一
田中一光 田中紀之 仲條正義
永井一正 福田繁雄 舟橋全二
松井桂三 松永 真 吉田カツ
'92年12月3日(木)—25日(金)
ggg
GINZA GRAPHIC GALLERY

289

OSAKA
AQUARIUM
RING OF FIRE
海遊館

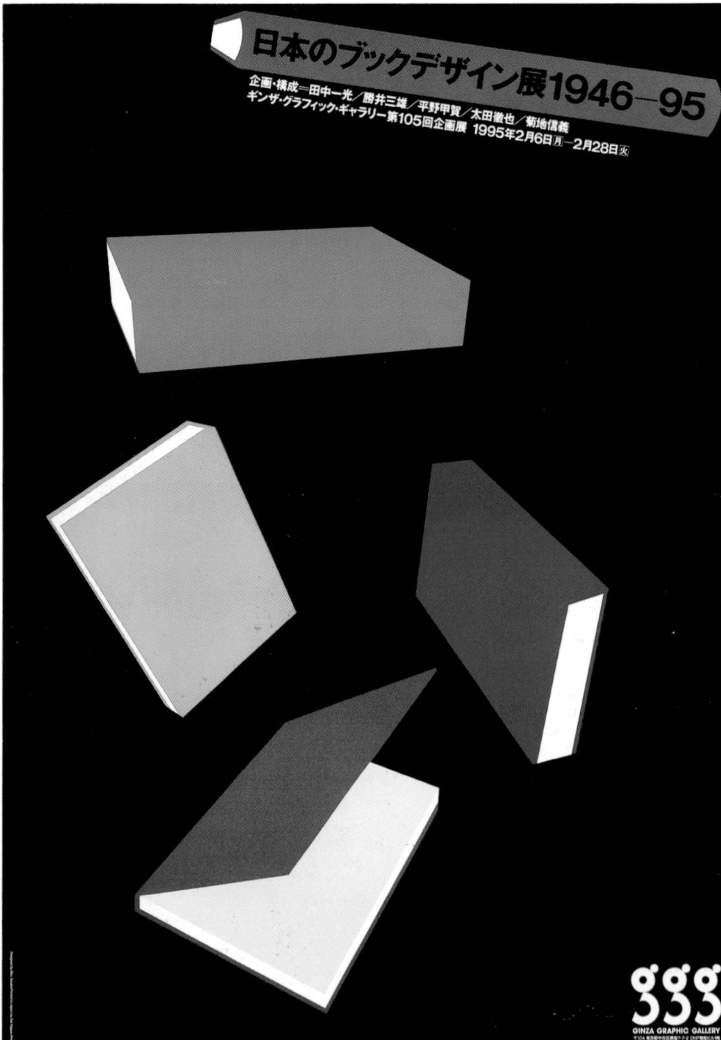
日本のブックデザイン展1946―95
企画・構成＝田中一光／勝井三雄／平野甲賀／太田徹也／菊地信義
ギンザ・グラフィック・ギャラリー第105回企画展 1995年2月6日(月)―2月28日(火)
GINZA GRAPHIC GALLERY

楽三百年

Man and Writing

Photo: Eiichiro Sakata

Ikko Tanaka was born in Nara City in 1930. He graduated from the Kyoto City College of Fine Arts in 1950. After working for Kanebo and Osaka Sankei Newspaper, Tanaka jointly established the Nippon Design Center, subsequently becoming its art director in 1960.

He established the Ikko Tanaka Design Studio in 1963. He directed the display design of the Government Pavilion (History of Japan) at EXPO '70, in Osaka, and the Oceanic Cultural Museum at Ocean EXPO '75, in Okinawa. He also produced and designed the "Japan Style" exhibition in London in 1980, and has been art director for Seibu Saison Group since 1973.

Tanaka held retrospective exhibitions at the Seibu Museum of Art, Japan; Cooper Union, New York; the Japanese American Cultural and Community Center, Los Angeles; Nara Prefectural Museum of Art, Japan; and the Musée de la Publicité, Paris.

His books include *The Work of Ikko Tanaka, Surroundings of Design, The Design World of Ikko Tanaka*, and *From the Desk of Ikko Tanaka*. He is a member of the Tokyo A.D.C. and of A.G.I. (Alliance Graphique Internationale), as well as director of the Japan Graphic Designers Association and a representative of Tokyo Designers Space. His works are held in the permanent collections of the Museum of Modern Art, New York, and the Stedelijk Museum, Amsterdam.

AWARDS AND HONORS

Received the Nissenbi Members' Award; Silver Prize at the International Poster Biennial, Warsaw; the Mainichi Industrial Design Award; the Recommended Artist's Award from the Ministry of Education, Japan; the Gold Award from New York Art Director's Club; the Award of Excellence from Tokyo A.D.C.; the Mainichi Art Award; and the Japan Cultural Design Grand Prize.

6

HENRYK tomaszewski

Proste ? proste

HENRYK TOMASZEWSKI

by SHOJI KATAGISHI, graphic designer

HENRYK TOMASZEWSKI IS KNOWN THROUGHOUT THE WORLD AS A GIANT IN THE FIELD OF POLISH POSTERS.

His posters are like pictures. As with many Polish posters, photosetting and photos are seldom used. The illustrations and letters are done lightly by the artist with a paintbrush or cut paper. His works have no exaggerated posturing or hardness. His relaxed drawings of figures, however, are not just swept up by cartoon techniques. His free, open form of expression has a feeling of dignity and intellect that emerges above and beyond the feat of rigorous hand labor. The drawn lines are refined, strong, and lyrical, and the ample amount of space and colored sections sometimes reflect the traditional Japanese way of creating shapes.

Thomaszewski's compact, lucid, and lyrical works, as is the trend in modern design circles, always make one

reflect deeply on the perfection of technique, meaningless extravagance, and the flood of excessive consumerism. His way of working and the expediency of his process make the most effective use of the candid aspects of illustrations to quietly restore the communication, the essence of conveying a message, that posters at one time had intrinsically.

While Tomaszewski has done a lot of work as an artist, he has also trained generations of graphic artists, painters, and designers in his role as professor of posters at the Warsaw Academy of Fine Arts. His unique method of teaching is legendary. He respects the individuality of his students; develops their sharp, analytical strengths and sense of humor; and shows them how to produce solutions to visual problems that take people by surprise. Drawn by his teaching methods, his many students come not only from Poland but from distant countries. Among them were Pierre Barnard, a member of the French Grapus, and Gérard Paris-Clavel. Tomaszewski's influence is very evident in their work, and the style they created is radically aggressive while being humorous and very playful. It is common knowledge that they had a revolutionary influence on French graphics.

Looking back over the past half century of Polish history, the intensity of the self-expression in Tomaszewski's works becomes evident. References to oppression and conflict were endlessly repeated as he confronted serious ide-

ologies such as nationalism, Catholicism, and communism. After all the sorrow, he must have put his own end to such troubles through his artwork.

Tomaszewski's works appear at first to be improvisations, but with time we can understand that they are the result of much observation and study. As he creates an image, his subject gradually ceases to be a means to an end, but becomes something with a much deeper meaning. He does not make a frontal attack on the system, but separates himself from any conflict with authority. He is very removed from the mentality of those in livery in addition to creating his personal image of a reality with poetic intervention.

He has the wisdom to see truth in the many fictions of reality as well as the ultimate understanding to see fiction as fiction. His passive, extreme caution itself is the beginning of free creativity; Tomaszewski has developed an unprejudiced visual language.

301

POLSKA
ROK
CHOPINOWSKI
1949
H.TOMASZEWSKI·49

Festiwal
Filmów
Radzieckich
dla Dzieci
i Młodzieży
29.X–4.XI.58
H.TOMASZEWSKI 58

MINISTERSTWO KULTURY I SZTUKI • CENTRALNE BIURO WYSTAW ARTYSTYCZNYCH
MOORE
Wystawa
rzeźb
Henry
Moore'a
H. Tomaszewski 59

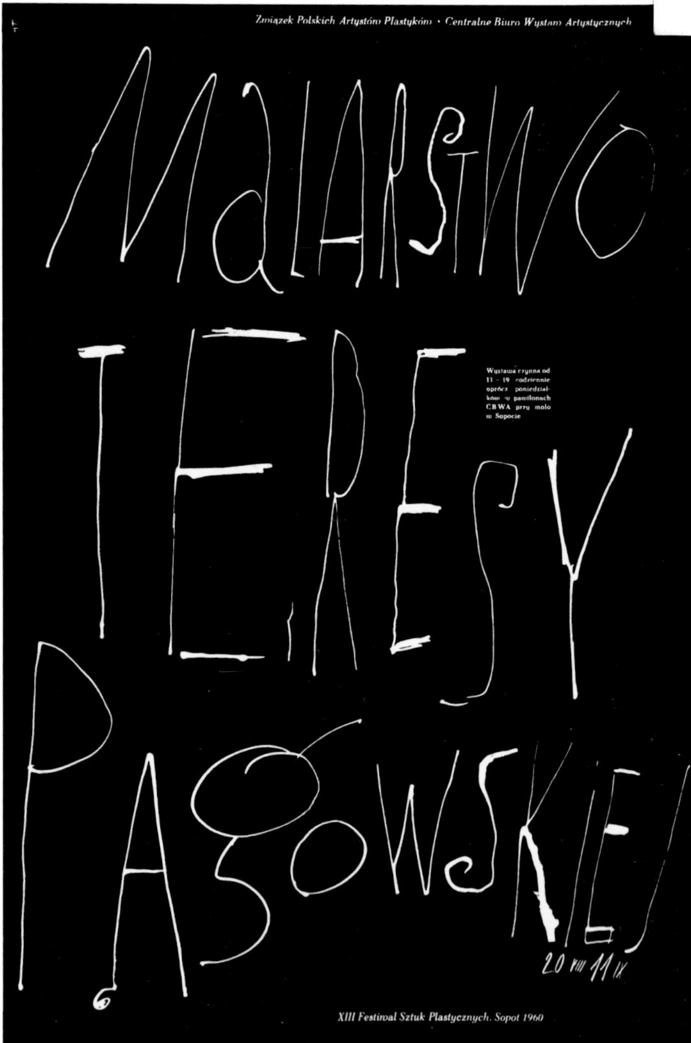
Związek Polskich Artystów Plastyków • Centralne Biuro Wystaw Artystycznych
MALARSTWO
TERESY
PAGOWSKIEJ
Wystawa czynna od 11 – 19 codziennie oprócz poniedziałków w pawilonach CBWA przy molo w Sopocie
20 VIII 11 IX
XIII Festiwal Sztuk Plastycznych. Sopot 1960

CYRK
ZJEDNOCZONE PRZEDSIĘBIORSTWA ROZRYWKOWE

Teatr Dramatyczny
KRÓL EDYP
SOFOKLES
TOMASZEWSKI 51

Opera Warszawska
Opowieści
J. Offenbach
Hoffmanna

CYRK
TOMASZEWSKI 65

FESTIWAL SZTUK RADZIECKICH I ROSYJSKICH 1967 R.
TEATR
Współczesny
Aleksander Ostrowski
PAMIĘTNIK SZUBRAWCA
WŁASNORĘCZNIE
Przez niego
napisany.

Teatr Powszechny
FANTAZY
J. SŁOWACKI

312

Henryk TOMASZEWSKI Varsovie
Société des Beaux-Arts Palais des Congrès
Kunstverein Kongresshaus Biel-Bienne (Foyer)
21 juin - 20 juillet 1969 21. Juni - 20. Juli 1969

Jazz
Jamboree 71
XIV Międzynarodowy
Festiwal
JAZZowy
Warszawa
28-30·X·1971
14th
International
Jazz Festival
Warsaw
October 28-30 1971

TOMASZEWSKI '72
TEATR
STUDIO
WITKACY

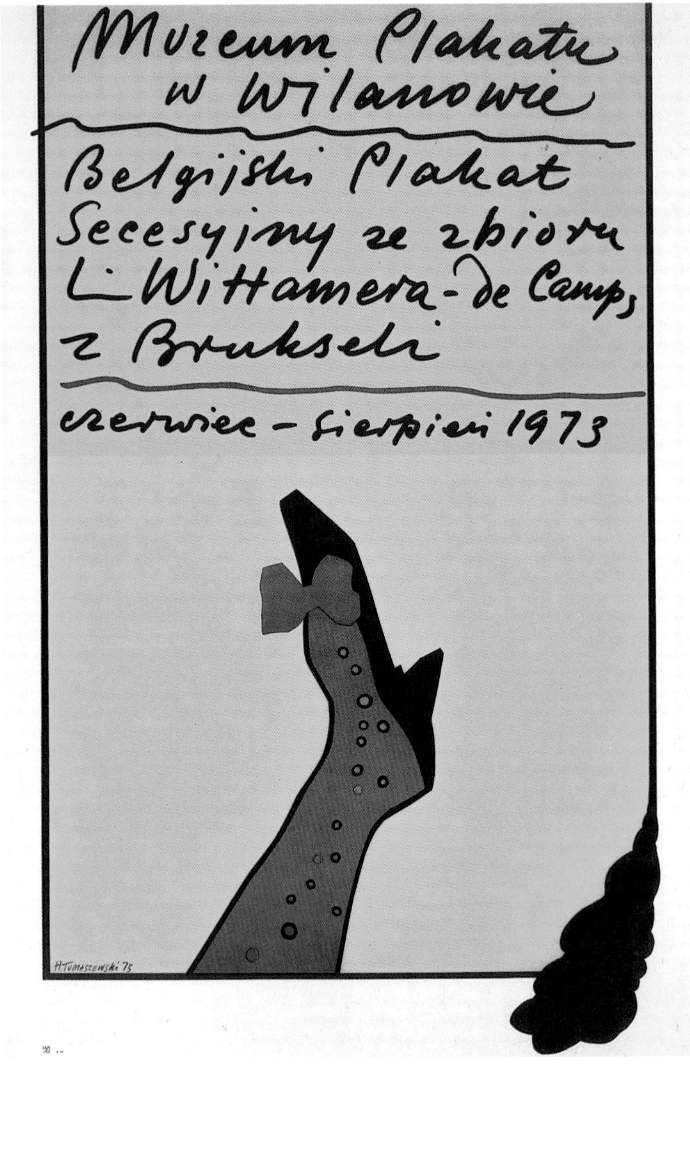
Muzeum Plakatu
w Wilanowie
Belgijski Plakat
Secesyjny ze zbioru
L. Wittamera-de Camps
z Brukseli
czerwiec - sierpień 1973
H.Tomaszewski 73

ŚLUB
W. GOMBROWICZ
TEATR DRAMATYCZNY

Varsovie
1975
THÉÂTRE
DES NATIONS
ENTRÉE

MARCH

1 MON
2 TUE
3 WED
4 THU
5 FRI
6 SAT
7 SUN
8 MON
9 TUE
10 WED
11 THU
12 FRI
13 SAT
14 SUN
15 MON
16 TUE
17 WED
18 THU
19 FRI
20 SAT
21 SUN
22 MON
23 TUE
24 WED
25 THU
26 FRI
27 SAT
28 SUN
29 MON
30 TUE
31 WED

Aleksander Fredro Damy i Huzary
Teatr TV
Kwadrat

50-ème Anniversaire de l'Union Internationale
de la
Marionnette

Teatr Powszechny Kordian Juliusz SŁOWACKI
H.TOMASZEWSKI - 80

H. TOMASZEWSKI. 81.
Peter Shaffer
Amadeusz
Teatr Na Woli

STANISŁAW TYM
TEATR NA WOLI
Pralnia

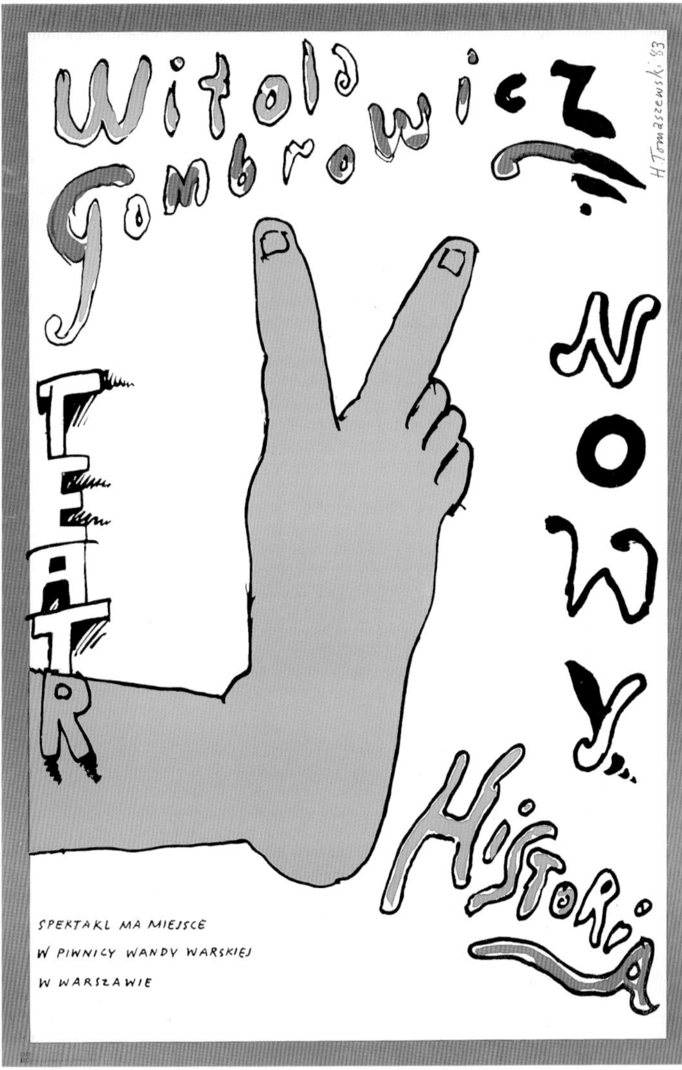
Witold Gombrowicz
Nowy Teatr
Historia
H. Tomaszewski 83
SPEKTAKL MA MIEJSCE
W PIWNICY WANDY WARSKIEJ
W WARSZAWIE

H Tomaszewski 83
26 th
INTERNATIONAL
FESTIVAL OF
CONTEMPORARY MUSIC
THE WARSAW AUTUMN
WARSAW
16 · 25 SEPTEMBER 1983

LEON KRUCZKOWSKI
NIEMCY
TOMASZEWSKI 87
Teatr Na Woli

Państwowa
Opera we Wrocławiu
Zbigniew
Rudziński
Manekiny
H. TOMASZEWSKI 85

Teresa
Pągowska
Wystawa
Malarstwa
Galeria Studio
Warszawa
Pałac
Kultury i Nauki
Czerwiec 1988

TEATR POWSZECHNY:
Bertolt Brecht
BAAL

Christopher
EDWARD II
Marlowe
H. Tomaszewski '86
TEATR NOWY
Warszawa

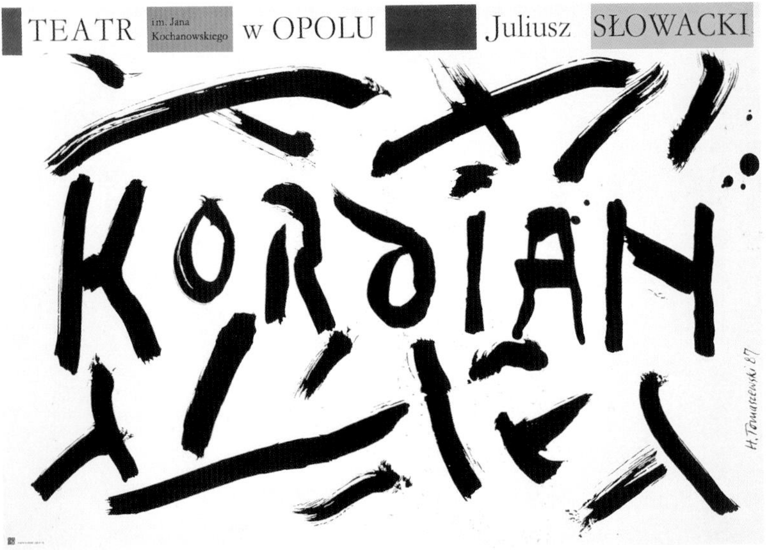
TEATR
im. Jana Kochanowskiego
w OPOLU
Juliusz
SŁOWACKI
KORDIAN
H. Tomaszewski '87

332

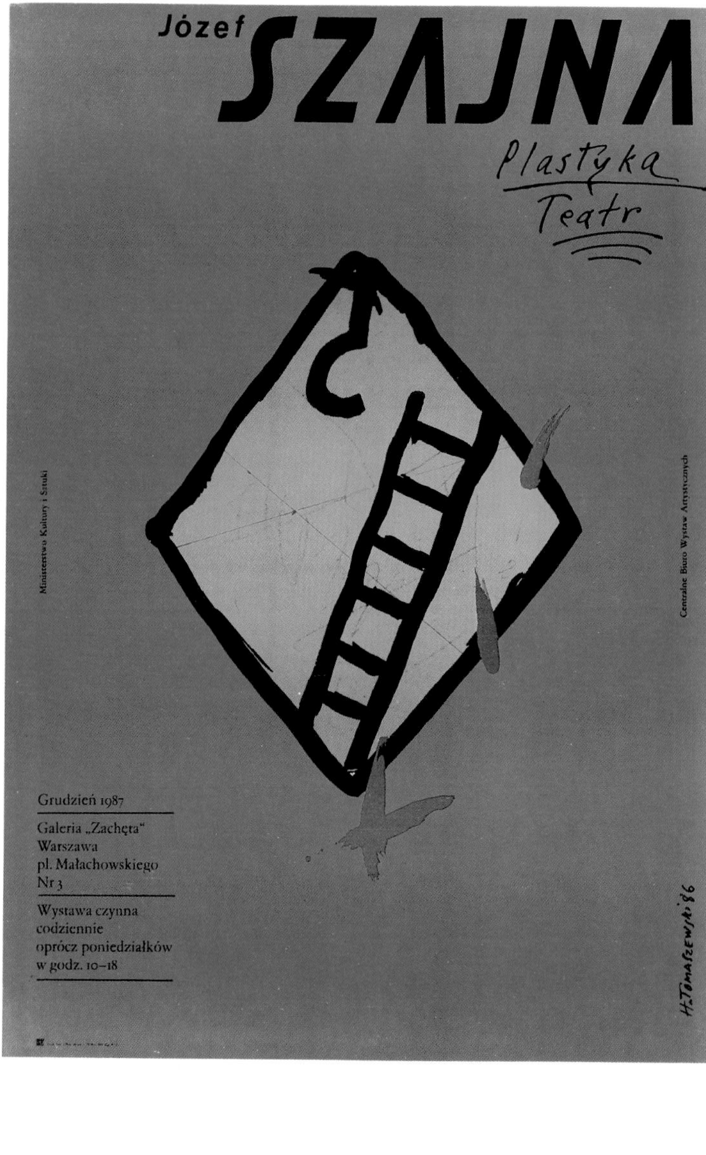
Józef
SZAJNA
Plastyka
Teatr
Ministerstwo Kultury i Sztuki
Centralne Biuro Wystaw Artystycznych
Grudzień 1987
Galeria „Zachęta"
Warszawa
pl. Małachowskiego
Nr 3
Wystawa czynna
codziennie
oprócz poniedziałków
w godz. 10–18
H. Tomaszewski '86

PLAKATY
PO PLAKACIE.
H. TOMASZEWSKI ·87·
BWA Leszno
Lipiec 1987
BWA Konin
Sierpień 1987
WYSTAWA
Z KOLEKCJI P.M. ZAŁĘSKIEGO

333

Ministerstwo Kultury i Sztuki
Centralne Biuro Wystaw Artystycznych
Akademia Sztuk Pięknych
Stowarzyszenie Polskich Artystów Grafików Projektantów
1923
1967
Wojciech
Zamecznik
Kwiecień 1988
Galeria ·Zachęta·
Warszawa, Plac Małachowskiego 3
Wystawa czynna oprócz poniedziałków w godz. 10-18
H. TOMASZEWSKI. 88.

LIBERTÉ EGALITÉ FRATERNITÉ
DANS LA PURE
BIOSPHÈRE
H. Tomaszewski.
Images Internationales pour les Droits de l'Homme et du Citoyen
ARTIS 89

H. TOMASZEWSKI.90
gitanes

POSTER
Galeria · Zachęta · Warszawa
pl. Małachowskiego 3
XIII
Międzynarodowe
Biennale
Plakatu
Warszawa
1990
Czerwiec
Sierpień
1990
13 th
International
Poster
Biennale
Warsaw
1990
Juni – august
1990
13th
XIII
Biennale
TOMASZEWSKI.90

Henryk Tomaszewski
Affiches tekeningen
LO
VE
Stedelijk
Museum
Amsterdam
20 april
tm 2 juni
1991
H. TOMASZEWSKI . 91.

338

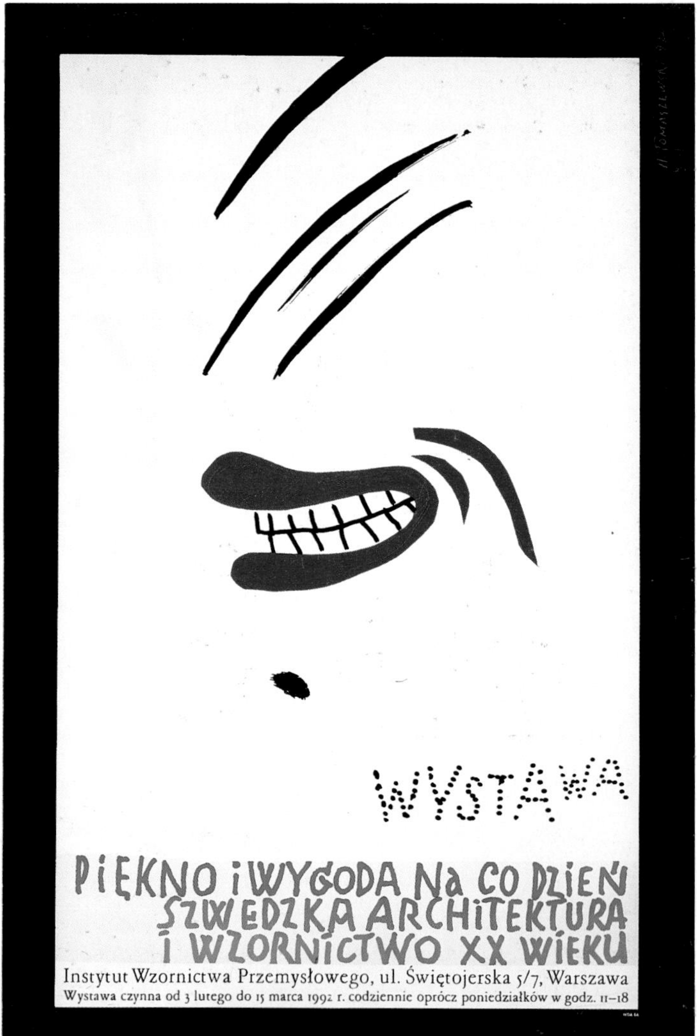
WYSTAWA
PIĘKNO I WYGODA NA CO DZIEŃ
SZWEDZKA ARCHITEKTURA
I WZORNICTWO XX WIEKU
Instytut Wzornictwa Przemysłowego, ul. Świętojerska 5/7, Warszawa
Wystawa czynna od 3 lutego do 15 marca 1992 r. codziennie oprócz poniedziałków w godz. 11–18

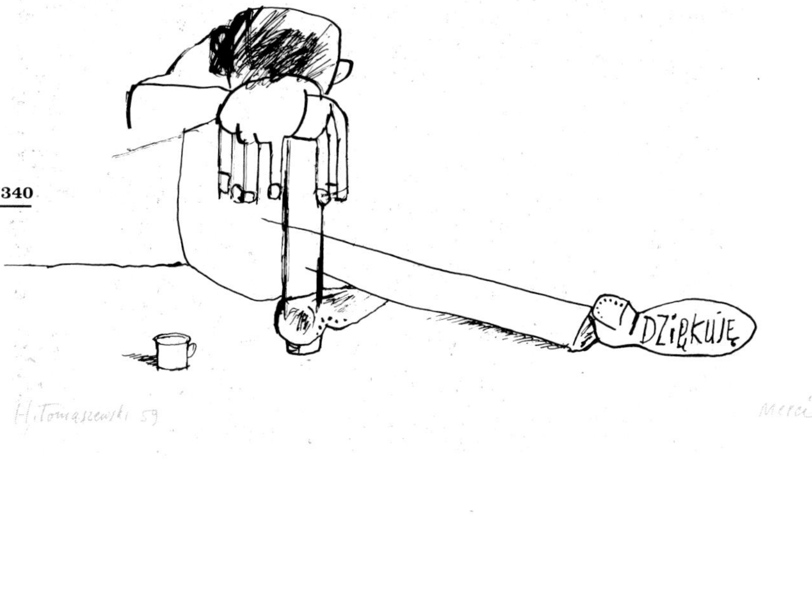
DZIĘKUJĘ
H. Tomaszewski 59
Merci

Plotka
Plotka
Plotka
Gossips

Wiosna
SPRING
H. Tomaszewski 59

H.Tomaszewski.

HOTEL

Leda

H. Tomaszewski 83

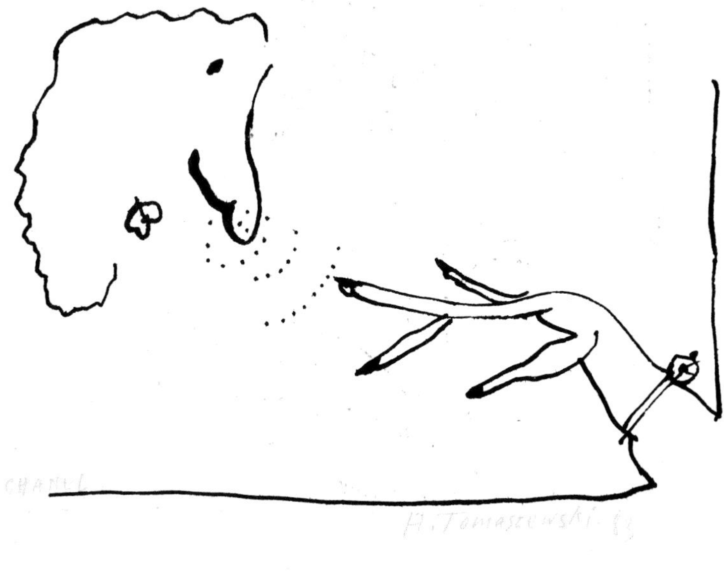
CHANEL
H. Tomaszewski

Oh dear, where are you?

H. Tomaszewski · 83

Henryk Tomaszewski was born in Warsaw, Poland, in 1914. He studied painting at the Warsaw Academy of Fine Arts from 1934 to 1939, and was a professor there from 1952 to 1985.

His work is represented in the collections of the Warsaw and Poznan National Museums, Poland; Muse de Arte Moderna, São Paulo, Brazil; Museum of Modern Art, New York; Villa Hugel, Essen, Germany; Museum of Modern Art, Kanagawa, Japan; Stedelijk Museum Amsterdam; Colorado State University; The Museum of Modern Art, Toyama, Japan.

AWARDS AND HONORS

First award for design of Polish Industrial Pavilion at New York World's Fair (1939). Five gold medals at International Poster Exhibition in Vienna (1948). National Award from Polish Government (1953). Polish Prime Minister's Award for illustration of children's books (1958). First Prize at 7th Biennial São Paulo, Brazil (1963). Gold Medal, Leipzig (1965). Gold Medal, International Poster Biennial in Warsaw (1970). Designated as Honorary Royal Designer for Industry, Royal Society of Arts, London (1979). First Prize, 3rd Poster Biennale in Lahti, Finland (1979). First Prize, Colorado International Poster Exhibition (1981). Alfred Jurzykowski Foundation Award, New York (1984). Special Prize, ICOGRADA (1986). Gold and Silver medals, Warsaw International Poster Biennial (1988). Bronze medal, Toyama International Poster Triennial, Japan (1991).

LIST OF

WORKS

SAUL BASS

18 SAUL BASS EXHIBITION–GRAPHIC AND FILM WORK
Announcement and poster, 1991

19 MAGNIFICENT SEVEN
Graphics for the film, 1960

20-21 THE MAN WITH THE GOLDEN ARM
Graphics for the film, 1995

22-23 BONJOUR TRISTESSE
Graphics for the film, 1958

24 SAINT JOAN
Graphics for the film, 1957

25 ADVISE AND CONSENT
Graphics for the film, 1962

26 ANATOMY OF A MURDER
Graphics for the film, 1959

27 EXODUS
Graphics for the film, 1960

28 GRAND PRIX
Graphics for the film, 1966

29 SUCH GOOD FRIENDS
Graphics for the film, 1971

30 VERY HAPPY ALEXANDER
Graphics for the film, 1980

31 THE TWO OF US
Graphics for the film, 1968

32-33 THE SHINING
Graphics for the film, 1980

34 CAPE FEAR
Frames from the title sequence for the film, 1991
In collaboration with Elaine Bass

35 GOODFELLAS
Frames from the title sequence for the film, 1990
In collaboration with Elaine Bass

36 SPARTACUS
Frames from the title sequence for the film, 1960
In collaboration with Elaine Bass

37 PSYCHO
Frames from the shower sequence for the film, 1960

38 FILMEX FILM FESTIVAL
Poster, 1985

39 10TH CHICAGO INTERNATIONAL FILM FESTIVAL
Poster, 1974

40 DIRECTORS GUILD OF AMERICA
Poster, 1968

41 65TH ACADEMY AWARDS
Poster, 1993

42 GAMES OF THE 23RD OLYMPIAD
Poster, 1984

43 COMMEMORATING THE CENTENNIAL OF THE FRENCH REVOLUTION: HUMAN RIGHTS 1789-1989
Poster, 1989

44 WARSAW SYMPHONY ORCHESTRA–WORLD TOUR
Poster, 1987

45 UCLA EXTENSION COURSES
Poster, 1992

46 PSYCHOLOGY
Book cover, 1987

47 PSYCHOLOGY–SECOND EDITION
Book cover, 1989

48-49 PSYCHOLOGY
Poster, 1993

50 STRATHMORE PAPER COMPANY
Cover for brochure, 1991

51 ROCKWELL INTERNATIONAL
Trademark, 1968

52 ALCOA
Trademark, 1961

53 CELANESE
Trademark, 1965

54-55 BELL SYSTEM
Trademark, 1969

56-57 AT&T
Trademark, 1984

58-59 UNITED AIRLINES
Trademark, 1974

60 LAWRY'S FOODS
Trademark and packaging, 1959

61 WARNER COMMUNICATION
Trademark, 1974

62 EXXON/ESSO
Worldwide gasoline service station design, 1981

63 THE BRITISH PETROLEUM COMPANY
Worldwide gasoline service station design, 1988

64 **(a)** KOSE COSMETICS
Symbol/trademark, 1991
(b) MINAMI SPORTS
Symbol/trademark, 1991

65 **(a)** KIBUN FOODS
Symbol/trademark, 1984
(b) MINOLTA CORPORATION
Symbol/trademark, 1978

66 (a) GIRL SCOUTS OF THE USA
Symbol, 1978
(b) UNITED WAY OF AMERICA
Symbol, 1972

67 JAPAN ENERGY CORPORATION
JOMO Service Stations
Symbol/trademark, 1993

IVAN CHERMAYEFF

71 MOSTLY MOZART, CONCERT PROGRAM, TOKYO
Symbol, 1993

74 PEACE CALENDAR
Calendar, 1958

75 TOWARD A SANE NUCLEAR POLICY
Book cover, 1957

76 MOBIL MASTERPIECE THEATRE 15TH ANNIVERSARY
Poster, 1985

77 INAUGURAL FLIGHT OF THE BOEING 747, PAN AMERICAN WORLD AIRWAYS
Menu cover, 1958

78 THE BOLSHOI BALLET
Poster, 1990

79 JACOB'S PILLOW DANCE FESTIVAL
Poster, 1993

80 TOMATO AND OTHER COLORS
Children's book, 1975

81 FACE VALUES, BY DAVID HENRY HWANG
Poster image, 1993

82 THE GHOST FACTORY, GRAMAVISION
Record album cover, 1988

83 SUN MOON STAR
Book, 1980

84 POLLUTION, THE AMICUS JOURNAL
Magazine cover, 1989

85 THINK, IBM CORPORATION
Magazine cover, 1989

86 THE BIG APPLE CIRCUS
Bus poster, 1988

87 (a) FISHY FACTS
Harcourt Brace
Children's book, 1994
(b) FURRY FACTS
Harcourt Brace
Children's book, 1994

88 PRIDE AND PREJUDICE
Mobil Masterpiece Theatre
Poster, 1980

89 COUSIN BETTE
Mobil Masterpiece Theatre
Poster, 1972

90 SUMMERGARDEN
The Museum of Modern Art, New York
Poster, 1979

91 SUMMERPIER
South Street Seaport Museum
Poster, 1980

92 DOCTOR FINLAY
Mobil Masterpiece Theatre
Poster, 1993

93 BETWEEN THE WARS
Mobil Showcase TV
Poster, 1977

94 DANGER UXB
Mobil Masterpiece Theatre
Poster, 1981

95 WAR AND PEACE
National Endowment for the Arts
Poster, 1977

96 WHITNEY MUSEUM OF AMERICAN ART
Poster, 1976

97 MINSTREL MAN, MOBIL SHOWCASE
Poster, 1976

98 LA BÊTE
Theater poster, 1979

99 M. BUTTERFLY
Poster/symbol, 1990

100 AMERICAN MUSEUM OF NATURAL HISTORY
Poster, 1984

101 THE ASCENT OF MAN
Mobil Masterpiece Theatre
Poster, 1974

102 THE SEARCH FOR ALEXANDER THE GREAT
Poster, 1982

103 WINSTON CHURCHILL: THE WILDERNESS YEARS
Mobil Masterpiece Theatre
Poster, 1983

104 INSTITUTE OF DESIGN 50TH ANNIVERSARY
Poster, 1988

105 THE UNIVERSITY OF CALIFORNIA, LOS ANGELES
Catalog cover, 1991

106 THE CORCORAN SCHOOL OF ART
Calendar, 1992

107 NINTH VAN CLIBURN INTERNATIONAL PIANO COMPETITION
Poster, 1992

108 THE SOPHISTICATED TRAVELER
The New York Times Magazine
Cover, 1993

109 IVAN CHERMAYEFF COLLAGES
Harry N. Abrams Publishers
Book cover, 1991

110-111 JACOB'S PILLOW DANCE FESTIVAL
Poster series, 2 of 4

112 KNOLL FURNITURE
Invitation, 1992

113 (a) EMPTY SUITS, GRAMAVISION
Record album cover, 1991
(b) BLUE MATTER, GRAMAVISION
Record album cover, 1989

114 (a) RHYTHM AND BLU, GRAMAVISION
Record album cover, 1989
(b) FIELDS, GRAMAVISION
Record album cover, 1989

115 (a) SHADOWS ON A WALL, GRAMAVISION
Record album cover, 1990
(b) SMART MOVES, GRAMAVISION
Record album cover, 1989

116 BLUE CORN
Mobil Oil Corporation
Tapestry, 1975

117 CACTUS FLOWERS
Mobil Oil Corporation
Tapestry, 1975

118 O TOWER
Mobil Oil Corporation, Research Headquarters, Pennington, New Jersey
Sculpture, 1984

119 FLYING RED O
Mobil Oil Corporation, Headquarters, Fairfax, Virginia
Sculpture, 1981

120 RING OF FIRE AQUARIUM, OSAKA
Mural, 1991

121 9 WEST 57TH STREET, NEW YORK CITY
Sculpture, 1980

122 NEW YORK SHOESHINE
Edward S. Gordon Company
Illustration, 1982

123 CAT FROM DEMELS
Collage, 1993

MILTON GLASER

127 ANGELS IN AMERICA
Created for Tony Kushner's Pulitzer Prize-winning Broadway play
Logo, 1993

132 TOMATO RECORDS, LTD.
Sketch for poster, 1967

133 FROM POPPY WITH LOVE
Poster, 1967

134 THE JUILLIARD SCHOOL
Sketch for poster, 1990

135 JUILLIARD IV, FLOWERS
Poster, 1990

136 THE JUILLIARD SCHOOL
Sketch for poster, 1989

137 THE JUILLIARD III, LADDER
Poster, 1989

138 THE CHT GROUP
Sketch for poster, 1995

139 RIMINI, ITALY
Poster, 1995

140 SCHOOL OF VISUAL ARTS
Sketch for illustration, 1977

141 SVA FLOATING MAN
Poster, 1977

142 NEW YORK TIMES
Sketch for illustration, 1991

143 NEW YORK TIMES GALLERY
Illustration, 1991

144 AMERICAN BAR ASSOCIATION
Sketch for poster, 1987

145 LAW
Poster, 1987

146 NEW YORK COMMISSION ON THE BICENTENNIAL
Sketch for poster, 1989

147 GEORGE WASHINGTON, 200TH ANNIVERSARY OF INAUGURATION
Poster, 1989

148 SILKSCREEN PRINT FOR STUTTGART
Sketch, 1975

149 GEOMETRICS
Silkscreen 1975

150 EXPO '92
Sketch for poster, 1987

151 SEVILLA 92
Poster, 1987

152 BROOKLYN COLLEGE OF PERFORMING ARTS
Sketch for poster, 1989

153 BROOKLYN COLLEGE OF PERFORMING ARTS
Poster, 1989

154 SAN FRANCISCO OPERA
Sketch for poster, 1981

155 CARMEN
Poster, 1981

156 LA GUARDIA COMMUNITY COLLEGE, CUNY
Sketch for poster, 1995

157 LAGUARDIA FLOWERS
Poster, 1995

158 DAVIDE-CAMPARI, MIRANO
Sketch for poster, 1992

159 CAMPARI BITTER
Poster, 1992

160 SOCIETY OF NEWSPAPER DESIGNERS
Sketch for poster, 1989

161 SOCIETY OF NEWSPAPER DESIGNERS
Poster, 1989

162 DOMUS MAGAZINE
Sketch for cover, 1993

163 DOMUS MAGAZINE
Cover illustration, 1993

164 PRINT MAGAZINE
Sketch for cover, 1993

165 PRINT MAGAZINE, NOVEMBER/DECEMBER
Cover illustration, 1993

166 GOGOL
Study for book illustration, 1987

167 NIKOLAI V. GOGOL
Used in Gogol Racconti de Pietroburgo
Publisher: Olivetti
Illustration, 1987

168 CONRAN'S
Sketch for poster, 1985

169 VIEW FROM AN ENGLISH COTTAGE INTO A FRENCH GARDEN WITH JAPANESE OBJECTS THROUGH AMERICAN EYES
Poster, 1985

170 ART DIRECTORS CLUB
Sketch for poster, 1987

171 ART DIRECTORS CLUB, CALL FOR ENTRIES
Poster, 1987

172 BOOK ILLUSTRATION
Study, 1983

173 THE COLLECTED WORKS OF APOLLINAIRE BOOK
Publisher: Andre Sauret
Art, 1983

174 LIGHTING FOR AURORA RESTAURANT
Study, 1986

175 AURORA RESTAURANT, NEW YORK CITY
Interior, 1986

176 SCHOOL OF VISUAL ARTS
Sketch for poster, 1994

177 SVA OLD/NEW
Poster, 1994

178 THE COOPER UNION
Sketch for poster, 1995

179 DESIGN TALK
Poster, 1995

180 WOLFTRAP
Sketch for poster, 1989

181 WOLFTRAP #3
Poster, 1989

PAUL RAND

185 SPARKLE AND SPIN
Book illustration, 1957

189 EXHIBITION, "THE GRAPHIC ART OF PAUL RAND"
Poster, 1957

190 ADC, INC. 3RD INTERNATIONAL EXHIBITION, NEW YORK
Poster, 1988

191 "DADA" WITTERNBORN, SCHULTZ, INC.
Book cover, 1951

192 ADVERTISING TYPOGRAPHERS ASSOCIATION
Poster, 1965

193 TRUE-ART-PRESS
Poster, 1978

194 INTERNATIONAL DESIGN CONFERENCE IN ASPEN
Poster, 1982

195 NEXT
Poster, 1986

196 UCLA EXTENSION COURSES
Poster, 1990

197 EXHIBITION "TOKYO AND OSAKA COMMUNICATION ARTS"
Poster, 1990

198 NEW YORK ADC "DESIGN '63"
Poster, 1963

199 IBM CORPORATION
Poster, 1968

200 STRAVINSKY
Book cover, 1968

201 DEATH MASK
Poster, 1968

202 AMERICAN INSTITUTE OF GRAPHIC ART
Book cover, 1968

203 IBM CORPORATION
Poster, 1981

204 IBM LOGOTYPE BOOK
Logotype, 1990

205 IBM LOGOTYPE BOOK
Logotype, 1990

206 IBM LOGOTYPE BOOK
Logotype, 1990

207 IBM LOGOTYPE BOOK
Package, 1990

208 PASTORE DEPAMPHILIS RAMPONE
Poster, 1987

209 TIPTON LAKES CORPORATION
Trademark, 1980

210 HELBROS WATCH COMPANY
Trademark, 1944

211 (a) COLORFORMS
Trademark, 1959
(b) CONSOLIDATED CIGAR COMPANY
Trademark, 1962
(c) AMERICAN BROADCASTING COMPANY
Trademark, 1962

212 WESTINGHOUSE ELECTRIC CORPORATION
TV billboard, 1961

213 UNITED PARCEL SERVICE
Trademark, 1961

214 WESTINGHOUSE ELECTRIC CORPORATION
Magazine advertisement, 1961

215 WESTINGHOUSE ELECTRIC CORPORATION
Magazine advertisement, 1954

216 WESTINGHOUSE ELECTRIC CORPORATION
Magazine advertisement, 1962

217 WESTINGHOUSE ELECTRIC CORPORATION
Magazine advertisement, 1961

218-219 NO WAY OUT
Twentieth Century Fox
24-sheets poster, 1950

220 CRESTA BLANCA WINE COMPANY
Magazine advertisement, 1946

221 DUBONNET CORPORATION
Magazine advertisement, 1954

222 OHRBACH'S
Newspaper advertisement, 1946

223 A BELL FOR ADANO
Alfred A. Knopf
Newspaper advertisement, 1945

224 WILLIAM H. WEINTRAUB & COMPANY, INC.
Newspaper advertisement, 1954

225 FRANK H. LEE CO.
Newspaper advertisement, 1946

226 ARENSBERG COLLECTION
Catalogue cover, 1957–66

227 CONTAINER CORPORATION OF AMERICA
Advertisement, 1946

228 LISTEN! LISTEN!
Harcourt Brace & World
Book illustration, 1972

229 LISTEN! LISTEN!
Harcourt Brace & World
Book illustration, 1970

230 LISTEN! LISTEN!
Harcourt Brace & World
Book illustration, 1970

231 I KNOW A LOT OF THINGS
Harcourt Brace & World
Book illustration, 1956

232 G. H. P. CIGAR COMPANY
Advertisement, 1953

233 VINTAGE BOOKS
Book covers, 1958

234 DIRECTION
Magazine cover, 1939

235 DIRECTION
Magazine cover, 1941

236 DIRECTION
Magazine cover, 1940

237 DIRECTION
Magazine cover, 1940

IKKO TANAKA

241 MAI
Graphic art, 1979

245 EXHIBITION, "WORLD GRAPHIC DESIGN"
Poster, 1959

246 NOH PLAY, "THE 5TH KANZE NOH"
Poster, 1958

247 NOH PLAY, "THE 8TH KANZE NOH"
Poster, 1961

248 NOH PLAY, "THE 27TH KANZE NOH"
Poster, 1980

249 NOH PLAY, "THE 28TH KANZE NOH"
Poster, 1981

250 TRADITIONAL PUPPET PLAY, "BUNRAKU"
Poster, 1966

251 THE 3RD INTERNATIONAL BIENNIAL OF PRINTS
Poster, 1962

252 CONTEMPORARY SCULPTURE EXHIBITION
Poster, 1972

253 CONTEMPORARY SCULPTURE EXHIBITION
Poster, 1978

254 EXHIBITION, "POSTER NIPPON"
Poster, 1972

255 EXHIBITION, "IKEBANA IKENOBO"
Poster, 1974

256 EXHIBITION, "IDENTITY"
Poster, 1975

257 PUBLICATION, "DESIGN OF IKKO TANAKA"
Poster, 1974

258 PYRAMID
Graphic art, 1973

259 DANCE TODAY '75
Poster, 1975

260 SEIBU THEATER OPEN
Poster, 1973
Illustration: Takahisa Kamijyo

261 BUTO RECITAL
Poster, 1973
Photograph: Hiroshi Yamazaki

262 JAPANESE PERFORMANCE
Poster, 1973

263 MUSIC TODAY '85
Poster, 1985

264 PUBLICATION, "DISCOVER KABUKI"
Poster, 1974

265 MUSIC TODAY '80
Poster, 1980

266 MORISAWA PHOTOTYPESETTING COMPANY
Poster, 1973

267 IKEBANA 100 MASTERWORKS
Poster, 1977

268 MORISAWA PHOTOTYPESETTING COMPANY
Poster, 1986

269 EXHIBITION, "CREATION OF SPACE"
Poster, 1982

270 SEZON MUSEUM OF ART
Poster, 1989

271 GINZA SAISON THEATRE
Poster, 1986

272 I&S ADVERTISING AGENCY
Poster, 1986

273 JAPAN CREATIVE
Package design, 1985

274 SALES PROMOTION, "CIAO ITALIA"
Poster, 1986

275 HAATH
Poster, 1986

276 MORISAWA PHOTOTYPESETTING COMPANY
Poster, 1986

277 THE 16TH ALL JAPAN NEW TALENT
DYEING AND WEAVING EXHIBITION
Poster, 1992

278 HANAE MORI
Poster, 1978

279 EXHIBITION, "IKKO TANAKA AFFICHISTE"
Poster, 1988

280 NATIONAL CULTURAL FESTIVAL
Poster, 1986

281 NIHON BUYO PERFORMANCE
Poster, 1981

282 JAPAN
Poster, 1986

283 HIROSHIMA APPEALS
Poster, 1988

284 IKKO TANAKA GRAPHIC ART EXHIBITION
Poster, 1988

285 IKKO TANAKA GRAPHIC ART EXHIBITION
Poster, 1990

286 PURPLE IRIS
Mural, 1992
21 1/2 x 27 feet

287 RED AND WHITE CAMELLIA
Mural, 1992
21 1/2 x 27 feet

288 PUBLICATION, "OSOROSHII AJI"
Poster, 1992

289 EXHIBITION, "FUROSHIKI"
Poster, 1992

290 OSAKA AQUARIUM
Poster, 1990

291 EXHBITION, "BOOK DESIGN IN JAPAN, 1946-95"
Poster, 1996

292 EXHIBITION, "SHARAKU 200 YEARS"
Poster, 1995

293 MAN AND WRITING
Poster, 1995
Photo: Takashi Hatakeyama

HENRYK TOMASZEWSKI

297 OKAY? OKAY
Poster, 1982

301 FOOT-BALL
Poster, 1948

302 CHOPIN YEAR 1949
Poster, 1949

303 FESTIVAL OF RUSSIAN CHILDREN'S FILMS
Poster, 1958

304 HENRY MOORE EXHIBITION
Poster, 1959

305 EXHIBITION OF PAINTING BY TERESA PAGOWSKA
Poster, 1960

306 CIRCUS
Poster, 1961

307 OEDIPUS REX
Poster, 1961

308 THE TALES OF HOFFMANN
Poster, 1962

309 CIRCUS
Poster, 1965

310 DIARY OF A ROGUE, ALEKSANDER OSTROWSKI
Poster, 1967

311 FANTAZY
Poster, 1967

312 HENRYK TOMASZEWSKI WARSAW
Poster, 1969

313 JAZZ JAMBOREE '71
Poster, 1971

314 WITKACY
Poster, 1972

315 BELGIAN ART NOUVEAU
Poster, 1973

316 WEDDING
Poster, 1974

317 THEATRE DES NATIONS-ENTREE
Poster, 1975

318 CAT, CALENDAR-MARCH
Poster, 1975

319 LADIEN AND HUSSARS
Poster, 1977

320 50TH ANNIVERSARY OF THE INTERNATIONAL UNION
Poster, 1978

321 KORDIAN
Poster, 1980

322 AMADEUS
Poster, 1981

323 LAUNDRY
Poster, 1981

324 HISTORY
Poster, 1983

325 26TH INTERNATIONAL FESTIVAL OF CONTEMPORARY MUSIC
Poster, 1983

326 GERMANS
Poster, 1984

327 MANNEQUINS
Poster, 1985

328 EXHIBITION TERESA PAGOWSKA
Poster, 1986

329 BAAL
Poster, 1986

330 EDWARD II
Poster, 1986

331 KORDIAN
Poster, 1987

332 EXHIBITION JOZEF SZANJNA
Poster, 1987

333 EXHIBITION POSTERS FROM THE M. ZALESKI COLLECTION
Poster, 1987

334 EXHIBITION WOJCIECH ZAMECZNIK
Poster, 1988

335 LIBERTY, EQUALITY AND FRATERNITY
Poster, 1989

336 GITANES
Poster, 1990

337 13TH INTERNATIONAL POSTER BIENNALE, WARSAW
Poster, 1990

338 HENRYK TOMASZEWSKI, LOVE, EXHIBITION
Poster, 1991

339 BEAUTY AND COMFORT IN EVERYDAY LIFE
Poster, 1992

340 THANK YOU
Poster, 1959

341 GOSSIP
Poster, 1959

342 SPRING
Poster, 1959

343 HOTEL
Poster, 1960

344 HIS MASTER'S VOICE
Poster, 1982

345 SNIFFLE
Poster, 1983

346 CHANEL
Poster, 1983

347 LEDA
Poster, 1983

348 NO TITLE
Poster, 1983

349 OH DEAR, WHERE ARE YOU?
Poster, 1983

6 CHAPTERS in DESIGN